*Praise for **You Were Bo...***

MW01063349

*"**You Were Born Wow** is a great reminder that all of us have the potential to rise, even in difficult circumstances. In her book, Katia takes us on a journey through storytelling as well as practices to live a life of pure abundance. Definitely a great refresher for reminding ourselves that we are empowered beings."*

Michelle Tanmizi
Best Selling Author of *Late Dawn* & Co-Author of *Adventures in Manifesting: Conscious Business*

"Katia Stern is indeed a WOW woman. Her desire to mentor and coach women towards empowerment reflects many principles I discuss in my own book. She is an inspiration for all of us to keep the flame of resilience alive in every aspect of our lives. Definitely a must-read. Follow Katia's practices and begin to feel life unfold through the power of manifestation."

Natalie Glebova
Former Miss Universe and Best Selling Author of *I Am Winning: A Guide to Personal Empowerment*

"Very motivating book! Katia inspires women to start living the life of their dreams. She gives them hope that it's never too late to begin their transformational journey. On the one hand, she is very serious with her message, but at the same time, she's funny with the way she presents it. As an athlete, I appreciate her discipline and devotion to her goals. She is a true inspiration for women of all ages and nationalities."

Natascha Ragosina
Professional Boxer

"*There was never a better time to triple on your strengths and turn your dreams into reality! Ladies, you have everything you need to become WOW inside of you. Read Katia's journey and follow her teachings to elevate your spirit and be the Star in your own movie. Following her example, anyone can turn their life into a vibrant and fulfilling experience, full of love and joy.*"

Irina Cheva
International Best Selling Author of *How to Create Your Multimillion Dollar Business with Ease*

KATIA STERN

You were born
WOW

Hasmark
PUBLISHING
INTERNATIONAL

Editor: Pashmina P.
pashmina@hasmarkpublishing.com

Book Design: Anne Karklins
anne@hasmarkpublishing.com

Photographer: Amer Mohamad

ISBN 13: 978-1-989756-05-8
ISBN 10: 1989756050

To my Mom and Dad, simply for the fact I was born Wow.
To my daughter who's confirmed that.
To all the haters who have become my free mentors.
To all the lovers who empowered me.

TABLE OF CONTENTS

CHAPTER 1

What if YOU Are a Wow Woman?

Ever since I was little, I was in search of an answer to what seems to be an easy question: What does it mean to be a great woman – a woman whose model of behavior, appearance, occupation, way of life and philosophy of thinking would suit me the most? A woman I'd want to be like, whose life and activities would inspire and motivate me? On my quest to find that woman, I looked closely and tried on all possible options.

Some traits resonated with my inner world. Some, though admired by society, I had a strong and rather irritating negativity toward.

The concept of a Wow woman came up after a long and rather painful search for the answer by self-studying, by examining others, by trial and error, and by wins and disappointments (with a couple of near-death experiences).

Having not found that one Wow woman I could relate to, I decided to come up with one. I took all the best traits and features from those I liked and admired to create the Wow woman – the one I would, ideally, want to become myself. I began to work on myself, trying to get as close as possible to that Wowness. Not to say that I ever reached that goal, because it's never-ending work: hard work. It's not easy, and it's quite often painful, but the work itself is absolutely doable. After all, nothing can stop a Wow woman when there's a pretty motivating goal to be happy, right?

Some results of my own work inspired others who had forgotten they were born Wow. I felt like I had a mission to help those who'd given up. I created my "Stern System" to assist those in need, and there are lots of them; lots of us, I should say. It doesn't matter if we're over 40 or not. We oftentimes feel like life is passing us by and there's so much we haven't done, haven't tried, and haven't achieved. We feel useless, invisible, unsexy and unattractive. We've invested ourselves in children, careers and husbands to the point that we've forgotten our own needs and deep desires. We feel guilty that we actually want something for ourselves.

As a child it seemed to me that at 45, I'd already be old and retired. Society in Russia, where I grew up, perceives this age range as an "older" woman. People look at how time has changed an actress (not for the better) and judge her for it, as if there was something she could have done to avoid the natural process of aging. For some strange reason, I thought this would never happen to me. I thought I wouldn't age. I wonder if you, my reader, had such thoughts? Or was it just my ego that was especially vain?

From the age of 17, I lived in Canada, the States and Europe. Here, in North America, it's a little different. Women are accepted by society as being "mature," or as I like to call it, "more experienced." We get more respect and attention. Nevertheless, the fears of aging are the same.

Generally, no matter where you are, a lot of women our age feel like they haven't lived a fulfilling life. There's so much suffering, so much pain. The middle age crisis in men is well known: your man bought a red Ferrari or a motorcycle, put on distressed jeans and dyed his hair. To me, men dying their hair to cover the grey signs of aging is so unappealing. (Unless he is Tony Robbins, of course). Only a beer belly could be more of a turnoff. Then your man goes on a "long business trip" with a "business partner" – usually a young, long-legged secretary who loves him so sincerely, not for his money and position, but for his heart and soul. She's very understanding and supportive, unlike you, his wife, who is demanding and selfish.

Or he left to go off in search of himself. Ever seen those men over 45 who put on pants that look like a skirt or brutally ripped jeans with hairy knees, and top it off with shaved heads? It's not clear who he is now: a yogi, a former drug addict, or a philosopher who finally found the meaning of life. He would never tell you that meaning because you would never understand. You're not at that high level of spiritual development. And that blonde, by the way, may also be by his side. She can get that philosophical meaning because, I remind you, she is supportive and understanding (and she can also fetch his high blood pressure, low cholesterol and stress relief pills if needed).

For men, this behavior, for some reason, is considered normal. It's accepted. We all know his middle-age crisis, like everything else, shall pass.

And even though we are not as unconditionally loving and tolerant as the secretary, we will understand – and, most likely, forgive.

The middle-aged woman's crisis, on the other hand, is less known and researched. It's like it doesn't exist. It reminds me of how we were told that there was no sex in the USSR. No sex: no problems. So, there's no crisis.

If the wife says to her husband of 20 years that she's unhappy or unfulfilled, at best, he will say, "Go have fun shopping!" Hopefully he sends her to Milan or Paris, but most likely she's off to the local mall for some Boxing Day sale. In the worst-case scenario, he may tell her to shut up or threaten her (Oh my God!) with divorce.

Most often, the story beforehand is that she's a housewife. Taking care of children is her entire life. She's so busy feeding, dressing, cleaning, going to school meetings, helping with homework, and taking them to hockey and ballet that she has no time for anything else. According to her husband, she does nothing. In reality, though, there's no time or energy to invest in herself. She's getting used to the idea that she's only a mother, and mothers aren't supposed to have needs. She's making sure the needs of others are being met. She's blocking the idea that she was born Wow – at least for a while. It will haunt her later, for sure. It always does.

All children have one common feature: they grow up and leave the parents' nest, no matter how good and cozy it was. Very often, the husband has also left this nest a while ago, but she didn't even notice that. She was busy playing the "I am a mother" role. As she was going through this phase, she did her "plus 20"; she added 20 kilograms to her body and 20 years on her face.

Or, the scenario could be that she's very successful in her career, busy making money and rapidly moving up the ladder: recognition, money, independence.

But suddenly, she's starting to lack strength and energy for this work. Career growth is not so motivating anymore; she really wanted to paint nature or sing carols all her life. The independence she strived for her entire career becomes a burden, and she questions whether it was needed in the first place.

It doesn't matter whether these or some other scenario is yours. You may have some of the following symptoms: you're bored, you feel useless or invisible, life has lost its meaning, or you're anxious, dissatisfied, therefore, overwhelmed. You may feel unrealized potential in in something. More often than not, you don't even know what that something is.

In your search for solutions, you change jobs, partners, and places of residence. You are obsessed with shopping, eating or drinking, or you have other obsessions with something or someone.

You may feel sad and lonely. You may feel as if you don't even exist. You blame yourself for not having achieved much and feel guilty for not having done more, but realize it may be too late and all there is in life is already behind you. I know – it sounds scary, doesn't it?

If not, then I congratulate you! I celebrate with you and am waiting for your advice on achieving such a beautiful state!

But if you answered yes to at least a couple of the above questions, then congratulations — you're going through a mid-life crisis!

What is there to rejoice about when you want to cry in your pillow?

Despite the fact that the crisis is a very difficult and

painful process, the good news is it can serve as a bell, an alarm – and sometimes a very loud one – that something needs to change urgently. This call is very necessary for most of us to begin rethinking our life, to reinvent ourselves into a new and improved woman who's successful and happy: a WOW woman!

I meet a lot of younger, not so "experienced" women, who, sometimes at 25, sometimes after 30, begin to feel the upcoming end of their youth. I honestly thought they'd invent some anti-aging drug and I'd never age. Apart from anti-cellulite creams that don't work, they haven't created anything. Much younger women also fear the end of their youth. I think the innate fear of aging is based on our ability to have children. When we lose the ability to conceive, we lose that youth. It's different with men. Maybe that's why they don't care about aging as much. They can (at least hypothetically), have kids at 60, 70, or even 90.

So, younger women face similar fears. I feel like it's more fear of the unknown. But the question is the same: is that it? Is that all there is?

Oh, you haven't become everything you wanted to become by 30? Is it too late to start a new relationship? New profession? New country, perhaps? Of course, to us, with more practice in life, this seems funny. I think of youth as a flaw that passes rather quickly. But not to the young ones; they think of it as a disaster, and so, they also want their Wow as soon as possible.

Who is that Wow woman? For me, this is a collective image, when every part of life is brought to the best possible level. Naturally, this process is endless; it lasts a lifetime. This is growth: spiritual, physical, material. It's never-ending – an eternal, permanent improvement of myself and the world around me. It's a cycle that includes vision, decision, action, satisfaction from the results, celebration, and then new vision and new results.

The life of any woman consists of different aspects. Each of them is a separate, small life by itself, with its own goals and objectives, achievements and difficulties, disappointments and successes. But, no matter how independent, one must understand one very important thing: these aspects overlap and influence each other.

If a woman feels uncomfortable in her own body, she's unhappy with herself, so her self esteem and self-confidence plummets. As a consequence, this often affects her career and finances. I won't even mention the idea of sex with that handsome co-worker, or (why not?) gardener. This is out of the question because she's not comfortable with herself, and no matter how hard this good-looking gardener tries to make her feel sexy, it can't work.

You get the message: it's all related and should be improved as soon as possible. The best way to start to do this is to start with your own body, because for a woman, her body is like home – like a sacred temple. If it's not in order (if it's not clean and tidy), she won't have the satisfaction she hungers for. The body-first approach worked for me, and it's working for my Wow clients who I coach on getting their Wow back.

I, myself, got that Wow back when I allowed myself to dream a little bigger. Bob Proctor, who I admire and consider my coach, always says, "Make a decision. The second you make a decision, everything starts to happen." Really, that's the most important thing we can do for ourselves. Even before meeting Bob personally, I made one of my best decisions. At 42, I decided to forget everything I learned that was considered "proper" and imposed on me from school, my parents and society. As Bob would say, I changed my paradigm. I started living by a new rule –the "What if?" rule. What if there's an answer to my questions on the other side of some crazy idea? What if there's happiness and satisfaction? So now I have taught myself to listen carefully to those risk-taking thoughts, and I act on them. The results are always a win just because it's better to do something than regret not having done it later.

I'm a girl with "mileage." This 46-year-old road trip with all its difficulties and setbacks is my experience; my most valuable and cherished asset. With my expertise, I feel like I have a mission to help you get your WOW back!

In this book, you'll understand what's stopping you from getting the life you really want. What is it that stands between you and your Wow that's causing you so much pain? I'll also give you simple and easy-to-follow steps to help you cure this pain. You'll have to do very little, but you will have to do it.

This is my Stern System to help you get your WOW back. Stern means "star" in German. "Stern" in English means strict and demanding – and so is my system. To become a STAR, you have to be strict and demanding. Yes, I'll disappoint you right here: there's no "How to lose 20 pounds in 10 days without giving up chips and hamburgers" or "How to trick him into marrying you on the first date." Actually, I can train you on "How to lose a guy you are sick and tired of in one day," but first let's become Wow and get that guy in the first place.

The best example of a WOW woman I had was my closest friend, Zhanna. She was one of the best Russian singers and dancers. She was really modest and didn't like to be called a singer even though she was a great one. Zhanna called herself a performer and she was the sex symbol of Russia. She was a combination of Madonna's energy, J.Lo's dancing style and Beyoncé's sex appeal. She taught me a lot of very important lessons on what it is to be a real Star, and on how to be Wow. Zhanna was there, up in the sky, where all the stars hang out; and yet, she was so available, so here, so simple and human. From her, I learned how to deal with haters, journalists and other jealous and negative people. She taught me how to take care of my own needs without jeopardizing the needs of the people around me. Zhanna had real priorities. She learned not to care about things that weren't essential and took action on the important goals that resonated with her values. She valued people and people loved her back. She found beauty in everything she saw and everyone she met. She would oftentimes say to me, "Katia, look how beautiful this girl is." I didn't see the beauty right in front of me. However, she did; she was the beholder and she saw it everywhere.

She had everything she could possibly dream of – fame, money, looks, attention – but she didn't have anything. She didn't have real love. She wanted to be loved unconditionally. Not as a girl from, as she put it, the TV or stage, but as a real woman – as the Wow woman that she was.

Zhanna always dreamed of having a child, and finally, she met somebody and gave birth to a beautiful son. Tragically, she enjoyed only three months of that pure happiness with her son before being diagnosed with brain cancer. She died two years later. Even through chemotherapy and other treatments, she remained positive and strong. I was ready to give up just by looking at her, but she was planning her future. Her life and death have had a great impact on my life. Even to this day, I often make a decision based on what I believe she would say about it, how I think she'd behave in the situation and how she'd react. I listen to her and feel gratitude for having this gift from God in my life.

With this gratitude for my own experiences, it's my desire, my plan, and my mission, if you will, to remind you that we all were born Wow!

If you believe and trust me, I can become your support, your source of information, and that magical kick in your not-so-perfect butt to get it moving and make your life easier, even before we start. Believe me, it doesn't have to be perfect. (Your ass, that is). By the way, I will be mentioning this special body part a lot in this book in real and figurative speech. If you have moral issues with that, you're free to close the book and I will gladly refund your money.

Wow is not about perfection. Wow is about the freedom to do what we want, feeling satisfied with everything we choose to do, and the joy of sharing our Wowness with the world!

So, are you ready to start living? Are you ready to allow yourself to become Wow and live the life you want?

If you said yes, put aside your existing beliefs and paradigms. Try learning to believe in "What if?": "What if whatever she's sharing is true and can work for me? What if? What if?"

WOW WOMAN ACTION STEP 1

In this chapter, I have explained what Wow means to me. I have described my own outlook on the traits and values that I think a Wow woman should have. Even though we are similar, we are quite different. We differ in our backgrounds, our childhoods, our paradigms, values, ideas and goals. You are not me and I am not you. So, I would like you to think of what that Wow woman is for you. I know how difficult it is to try to come up with these qualities. I'm here to make your life easier, so I've offered you some ideas. Choose your own description and create your Wow you.

Here is a list of some Wow personality traits. Please check 10 characteristics that you already possess and 10 that you would like to add to your Wowness. Really own the ones you have now. Revel in them, and step into the new ones.

☐ 1. Active
☐ 2. Admirable
☐ 3. Adventurous
☐ 4. Amiable
☐ 5. Ambitious
☐ 6. Aspiring
☐ 7. Athletic
☐ 8. Attractive
☐ 9. Balanced
☐ 10. Brilliant
☐ 11. Calm
☐ 12. Captivating
☐ 13. Caring
☐ 14. Charismatic
☐ 15. Charming
☐ 16. Cheerful
☐ 17. Clever
☐ 18. Compassionate
☐ 19. Confident
☐ 20. Considerate
☐ 21. Courageous
☐ 22. Creative
☐ 23. Dedicated
☐ 24. Deep
☐ 25. Disciplined

☐ 26. Dynamic
☐ 27. Educated
☐ 28. Efficient
☐ 29. Elegant
☐ 30. Energetic
☐ 31. Enthusiastic
☐ 32. Exciting
☐ 33. Extraordinary
☐ 34. Fair
☐ 35. Faithful
☐ 36. Focused
☐ 37. Forgiving
☐ 38. Friendly
☐ 39. Fun-loving
☐ 40. Generous
☐ 41. Gentle
☐ 42. Genuine
☐ 43. Glamorous
☐ 44. Gracious
☐ 45. Honest
☐ 46. Honorable
☐ 47. Humble
☐ 48. Humorous
☐ 49. Impressive
☐ 50. Intelligent

☐ 51. Intuitive
☐ 52. Kind
☐ 53. Logical
☐ 54. Lovable
☐ 55. Loyal
☐ 56. Mature
☐ 57. Moderate
☐ 58. Modest
☐ 59. Neat
☐ 60. Objective
☐ 61. Open
☐ 62. Optimistic
☐ 63. Organized
☐ 64. Original
☐ 65. Passionate
☐ 66. Patient
☐ 67. Peaceful
☐ 68. Perfectionistic
☐ 69. Persuasive
☐ 70. Playful
☐ 71. Polished
☐ 72. Popular
☐ 73. Practical
☐ 74. Precise
☐ 75. Profound

☐ 76. Prudent
☐ 77. Rational
☐ 78. Realistic
☐ 79. Relaxed
☐ 80. Reliable
☐ 81. Resourceful
☐ 82. Respectful
☐ 83. Responsible
☐ 84. Romantic
☐ 85. Secure
☐ 86. Self-sufficient
☐ 87. Sensitive
☐ 88. Sentimental
☐ 89. Serious
☐ 90. Sexy
☐ 91. Shrewd
☐ 92. Skillful
☐ 93. Sophisticated
☐ 94. Spontaneous
☐ 95. Strong
☐ 96. Tolerant
☐ 97. Understanding
☐ 98. Wise
☐ 99. Witty
☐ 100. Youthful

Which ones are the new you?

_____

_____

_____

_____

_____

_____

_____

_____

_____

_____

_____

_____

_____

_____

_____

_____

_____

_____

_____

_____

CHAPTER 2

WHY Your Way to Wow!

As she was standing there onstage half naked, wearing her sparkling Swarovski-covered diamond bikini, she thought about all the fake things: her fake diamonds, fake tan, fake lashes. She had always detested everything fake as much as those who wore them. She detested – or, in reality – was afraid of being judged by her looks and her body. To overcome that fear, she compensated through education. She graduated from two law schools and earned a psychology degree. She never stopped getting educated and became a self-development junkie. She did all of this simply to quiet her real desires and needs to shine and sparkle, to be on stage and feel like a star. She was longing for those lights, for the packed theatre full of men and women looking at her, applauding and screaming with admiration.

As it was, her jaw was trembling and her teeth were chattering. She tried to smile, as there was part of her that very much needed this 20 seconds of fame. Her legs were shaky, doing a tap dance in unison with her teeth. Her hair was so blonde and teased that she looked like a cross between Barbie and Brigette Bardot before she joined the animal rights movement. Both of them were beautiful, and so was she: perfect make-up, perfect body. Not-so-perfect ass. Far from perfect, to be honest.

The back pose was coming. *There's no way out of it. Okay, stomach in. Hold your breath. Don't let anyone know you're holding your breath. Keep smiling.* The right leg goes back, the left one moves to that point. She steps, turns and sticks out that butt. *And don't forget, there's that skin crease that serves as a reminder of the years of sitting on it.* Literally, there's a crease from spending years sitting in universities and jobs trying to avoid that need to be judged by her looks and having to prove to the world that, apart from the blue-eyed pretty face, she's a smart, well-educated woman. Figuratively, she's been sitting on it, waiting for somebody (preferably that royal prince), to knock at the door and say, "Here I am! It's the perfect day and the perfect time to finally start living the life you've been postponing until the right moment for so long! I'll take care of all your needs. I'll help you fulfill all your deep desires. There are no circumstances and no reasons not to start today. There are finally no life events happening, no distractions going on, and no financial issues – just lots of energy and motivation!"

Strangely enough, that day and that prince never came. Believe me, she was patient. She waited. To wait for 42 years is a damn long time to wait. Most give up. Most quit. But not her. She had a goal, and the goal was extremely compelling. She wanted to be Wow. She knew her WHY. She was me. She *is* me – the always striving for Wowness 45-years-young woman, mother to a teenage daughter, lawyer turned health coach, writer, and fitness bikini competitor at 42.

If you had told me this story a few years ago, I would have listened, believed half of it, and most likely wouldn't think it was about me. (Or I would've considered you out of your mind).

Ironically, it was me who seemed to be out of my mind to the people around me when they started seeing me behaving outside society's "norms." I was always training or going to/from the gym, rapidly losing weight, and carrying containers of food everywhere from a hockey game to a private plane. Those who didn't like me very much were gossiping about how fucked up in the head I was, how obsessed I was with the gym, and how unhappy I must have been. I had to be sublime with this hobby and just ignore it all. There was also a version that I was lacking sex and compensating for all of it with training. Of course, those who love me told me about all the gossip, but were worried themselves and carefully inquired if I was sick.

The truth is I never told anyone of my crazy, vicious plans. Almost nobody knew, and no one could even have guessed about my unrealistic ideas – not my mother, not my boyfriend, not my daughter, or even my best friend. I didn't need their support, but not because the people I love wouldn't support me. It was the opposite. I knew they'd try to stop me because their idea of support is to protect me from the unknown. They'd want me to be safe and secure. Instead, I'd only be sorry that I didn't reach for my dreams.

I need to mention my Wow man here. He was very understanding about it. I just asked him to trust me. I told him I knew what I was doing and I'd explain everything to him on the 9th of April. And so, he did. He trusted me and just let me do something that was really important to me – that was my Wow. Having a relationship where there's no need to explain and justify your needs and desires is a blessing. I think it's the main test of the quality of a trustworthy partner. You're simply accepted and loved for being the truth — the true you.

Actually, on the day of the contest, he didn't get an explanation; he got a photo. Thank God he's not very active on social media. I sent him a photo of me onstage. He's not an emotional guy, either. He simply replied, "Nice."

I was like, "Is that all you can say?" I was about to write back with anger when I got another message.

"But who is that?"

"Me, of course! Why would I send you a picture of another beautiful half-naked woman?" Us women don't do that. We're afraid to be compared and lose the competition round.

"WOW!!!" he said. For the unemotional him, that was quite a lot.

As for the others, I posted a picture of my wrist with a bracelet that said "Competitor" the day before the contest, as if I claimed it.

The next day I posted the stage photo and the trophies. As expected, the reactions were varied: everything from a lot of respect and heart-warming congratulations to people accusing me of Photoshopping my face onto somebody else's body.

With the new era of social media, our communication methods have changed. We don't have to call or write. We just open Instagram and Voilà! My daily routine is there. (By the way, my Instagram is @Katia_stern_). To show interest, we just follow or unfollow: like or unlike.

On the one hand it brings some transparency to our personal relationships. We lie less because we're scared to get busted on Facebook. But, on the other hand, we break up more if that bust happens.

We'll talk more later on the subject of support and the importance of your social circle. For now, I'm concentrating on the most important thing to help you get to your goal of reclaiming your Wow. For that, we need our Why – the reason, the purpose, the motivational factor, the why underneath the WHY. The Wow factor, as I call it.

I want to warn you beforehand, so that you don't make the mistake of trying to skip this most important step in getting your desired outcome. This is probably the number one mistake we make when we're trying to achieve something and don't succeed, and then we think of ourselves as failures. We don't want to be failures, right? So, the real reason for us to be doing something (the motivational factor, the Why), has to be so compelling that all other factors, excuses and circumstances become so tiny and so unimportant that you always stick to your goal.

Let me explain. The number one request I get from women is, "I want to lose weight. I tried all sorts of different fad diets and made an effort to exercise, but couldn't stick to it, so my weight loss goal didn't happen. I failed the diet. I quit exercising. I am unhappy; I gave up."

I'm not surprised. It's a standard outcome when we don't have a strong reason for doing something, or when the Why isn't strong enough. "Why do you want to diet?" I ask.

"Because I want to lose weight, of course," they answer, and look at me like I'm crazy. They don't understand I'm trying to get their why out of them. My next questions are usually: What does "dieting" mean to you? Describe what you think about that process. What are the associations? What are the feelings?

What we all feel about dieting is that it's deprivation and restriction. It's hard, stressful, harsh and unpleasant. All of that for losing a few kilos so that you can fit into a pair of jeans? Come on! That's not a strong enough reason to make me suffer. After all, I am a grown woman, independent and educated to behave in alignment with my free will. And I can afford a new and slightly bigger pair of pants! Also, by nature, we are hedonists. We seek pleasure. If there's no compelling reason, we don't want to suffer.

So, how do we lose weight, you ask? We need to find that Why to keep you motivated. We have agreed that you want to lose some of you in order to fit in those jeans, but I want to know how that will change your life. You lose the weight, and then what?

I had a client, a beautiful woman in her late 30s, who was quite successful in her career, but was not happy about her Wow. She felt like there was so much more she could do: get out of a toxic relationship, become more self-confident, and start public speaking, which would substantially advance her business.

I am convinced that for a woman, these changes absolutely have to start with body transformations. As we started working, she told me that if she could wear those white shorts she bought some time ago, she'd feel Wow again. Wearing those shorts became her vision, her Wow factor, because she said it would give her confidence. This confidence would empower her to make decisions based on self-love. She'd find the strength to quit that unneeded and totally destructive relationship. That same confidence coupled with self-respect would give her a new attitude and dramatically improve her business relationships. She'd expand her accounting business. And she did. She sent me the photo of herself wearing shorts and high heels – a combination she could never have dreamed of. As a bonus to this vibrant and fulfilling state, she had enormously upscaled her business. I doubt the motivation of losing weight brought her these changes. Instead, I say, it was the ability to figure out how these transformations would benefit her personal and professional life. This allowed her to let go of her distractions and self-sabotaging behavior. Every time she wanted to get off the plan, I would remind her of her Why, and she got right back into it simply because she knew all those changes would eventually make her happy. Plain and simple: your happiness is behind the transformation. When you compare having another piece of cheesecake to being happy, what are you going to choose?

I'm very proud of this particular story because it was one of the first in my practice. Then I realized: Oh my God! So many of us are suffering because we're not achieving our goals, when, in reality, we don't work enough on finding the Why first. And secondly, we simply forget it when we get too preoccupied with the completion of the action plan. What we most often need isn't another perfect diet or exercise regime (perfect anything doesn't exist, by the way). What we need is to remember our Why and our Wow. As your coach and friend, it's my job to always remind you that you're Wow. You were born Wow, but then forgot.

WOW WOMAN ACTION STEP 2

To help you achieve your own Wow factor, I'm offering you a few questions to answer. Please take some time to dig in to the real "Why" behind your obvious "why." It will give you some much needed clarity and help you find your biggest motivation so you'll keep moving towards your goal and the life you want (and definitely deserve).

FINDING YOUR WHY

Part 1

What's the outcome you really want?

If you could wave a magic wand and really get what you want when it comes to the way you look (and, more importantly, feel) in the next 90 days, what would that look like? Be specific. What will you be wearing? Where are you going to be? Will you feel light? Sexy? Confident? Think about it, see it, visualize it and live it! Imagine every possible detail. Try it on for feel. Listen to your body. Are you relaxed? Are you tense? Do you get goosebumps, maybe? What do you look like now that you are Wow?

_____

_____

_____

_____

_____

_____

_____

_____

_____

_____

_____

_____

Part 2

How will others see you?

_____

_____

_____

_____

How will they react? What will say say?

_____

_____

_____

_____

How will men look at you?

_____

_____

_____

_____

How will women stare at you?

_____

_____

_____

_____

Specifically, how will you feel better? Describe this.

_____

_____

_____

_____

_____

What kind of difference does this bring into your life?

_____

_____

_____

_____

_____

What does this difference feel like?

_____

_____

_____

_____

_____

How does it change your personal life? How far-reaching is it?

_____
_____
_____
_____
_____

How does it influence your professional life?

_____
_____
_____
_____
_____

How does it help your financial situation?

_____
_____
_____
_____
_____

How does it enhance your social life?

_____
_____
_____
_____

Now, write all the answers in a statement.

My WOW FACTOR is:

I want this… (describe what you wrote in Part 1), because when I achieve it, it will get me this… (insert everything from Part 2) and this will make me… (happy, complete, satisfied, etc.).

_____

_____

_____

_____

_____

_____

_____

_____

_____

_____

_____

_____

_____

_____

_____

_____

_____

_____

_____

On a scale from 1 to 10, how important is this to you?

_____

(Hint: if it's not 9 or 10, dig deeper into why you want this. Otherwise it's not important enough for you and you just won't do it or own it!)

Live it. Feel it. Enjoy it. I'm sure, you'll love your Wow. Admire yourself with love.

CHAPTER 3

Make your Decision: Get What You Want With Precision

As you can tell, I got my Wow back with that bikini competition in Los Angeles, almost in Hollywood. I wasn't looking to receive these great feelings of playing the main part in my own life story and being the Star of it so close to the Hollywood sign. It was just a coincidence that the most suitable dates for the competition were in L.A. But I don't believe in coincidence. As someone with two law degrees, I believe in laws: the Law of Attraction, in this case. I became interested in this whole concept when the movie *The Secret* came out in 2006. This movie was life-changing for me. The very notion of attraction states that everything you think about, see, hear, listen to, read, watch on TV, fantasize about and get emotionally involved in, you attract. Of course, it's almost impossible (especially for us women), not to get involved. It feels like we are programmed to react and experience some pain and suffering together with the news or movie characters. And so, according to the Law, we attract exactly what we are trying to avoid so much. On the contrary, if we focus on the positive, we start attracting joy and abundance into our lives. But that requires work and patience.

Of course, it was Bob Proctor who I remembered most from the movie. He looked like a grandfather to me; not because of his age, but because of his wisdom and wits. And the suit. My grandfather always wore a suit because he was a big shot – the director of a huge mill factory in Moscow. The mill was a strategic resource after World War II. When, by chance, there was food, flour and bread, this was considered an important resource to be distributed by special order. So, my grandfather wore suits, had a driver, and lived in the center of Moscow, right next door to the Red Square wall, close to Lenin's house and the Mausoleum. This building now serves visitors as the Four Seasons Hotel.

From that movie, I remembered that the rule of that Law is to first decide what you really want. Visualize the outcome and convince your conscious mind that you're already in possession of what you desire. When you move this thought into your unconscious through repetition, the universe will give you the instructions and means for the completion of this mission. Making the "right" decision is tough, though. We weigh and judge all possible out-comes. We doubt. We feel helpless. We strive for perfection in making the "proper" choice, without realizing that we can only know the outcome of that choice after we choose that very solution. The secret that most women don't realize is that the chosen path is always the right one, because when you made your decision, you based it on the resources and circumstances at that particular time. It was a conscious, sane decision, I hope. Nobody was holding you all chained up and forced you to make a decision. It was your free will. Now, looking back, you may not remember those circumstances and you tend to start fantasizing and creating a different memory for yourself, and end up regretting that made up reality.

One of the toughest decisions I ever had to make was leaving the father of my three-year-old with nothing but my daughter in my arms and the car keys. Actually, I also took an antique 50-pound bronze statue of a woman with wings. Now I think of her as a symbol of a Wow woman. At the time, I just couldn't stand the idea of leaving empty-handed.

You can try anything in your power to make a man happy, but if he doesn't have purpose, there's not much you can do. Men are born to achieve, to win and to conquer. Once they lose their hunt, that's it. They can't find their path to happiness. They may go into depression; more often into drinking and drugs. Of course, it can happen to women, too, but we usually adjust to situations like this much easier. Our happiness and self-worth may more often be found in our children, family and love life – at least for some of the time. Men may lose themselves easier if they don't find another prey to catch or another princess to save.

That was the case with my daughter's father. Having finished his sports career, he found himself in a new world where there was no sport and no achievements. He was a professional race car driver – and then one day, he wasn't. I don't know if people change. I think people, men or women, may choose to behave differently in new circumstances. They may be like this or that according to what's more important to them in a specific situation, so their values may change. And then their behavior changes, according to the new values. I think he'd decided to take a break from being disciplined, sober, active and responsible. He made a decision to play the bad boy.

A lot of professional athletes I know end up like this.

39

For years, they've been doing the same thing over and over – training, winning, losing, repeating. They were told what to eat, when to get up, who to fight and how to do it. They don't belong to themselves for many years. Their identity is wrapped up in the team or the sport, and that's why they get paid the big bucks. Their time is devoted to entertaining us and avoiding injury. His racing career was over, and so was he.

We'd met at a birthday party a few years prior. I wasn't even supposed to be at this party. It was absolutely by chance. I noticed him from the far end of the restaurant. He was alone. He was quiet; he was different. Very calm, masculine energy was emanating from him. He wasn't really my type. He wasn't too tall, and not extremely good-looking, but there was something real about him. He didn't drink or dance. He looked confident. I guess that's the trait which attracted me.

With the end of his career, his confidence vanished. He began drinking and partying a lot. It was awful, but not bad enough for me to leave him. I was patient, waiting for things to get better. Meanwhile, I started working for a large company as the head of the oil product sales department. I got up early, put on my suit and went to work. He stayed home in bed because there was nowhere to go. It was depressing for us both. I tried helping, but didn't have much success.

The situation had become totally unbearable when he hit me. He didn't punch me. It didn't get that far; I wouldn't allow that. He hit me with a huge bouquet of roses at our daughter's one-year-old birthday party. I guess if a Wow woman has to be hit, then at least it was done in style – with roses.

I thought I knew a lot about domestic violence. Ironically, I had written a term paper on "Why women stay in abusive relationships" when getting my BA in Psychology.

Interesting. Why had I picked that subject? I'd never experienced it in my family. I'd never seen anything like that in real life. Did I predict my future? Did I create it? I also took Italian and French classes back then, as I knew that I'd need these languages. I didn't know when and where, but my intuition told me to learn. Later, I lived in both Italy and Monte Carlo, where they speak lots of French.

In my paper, I wrote that women who stay in abusive relationships decide to be victims of circumstance. They're weak and too scared to take action. They choose this type of life. It's a decision they make. They decide to live like that and it becomes their new comfort zone. They adapt because of the fear that it could be worse. To be honest, I even felt some disrespect toward those who stayed and suffered. I knew that if they made a decision to be strong, to be in control of their own lives, that things would only get better. I had it all figured out.

But I didn't. I wasn't aware of one strong feeling; one compelling reason not to make that move. Now I was going through it myself: the guilt I'd have about raising my daughter without her father. That was probably the worst guilt I've ever experienced, but I knew it was impossible for me to continue living that way. It's totally not me to take the abuse. I felt like the decision to leave would be based on my selfish needs, not taking into account my daughter's feelings about not having a "normal," full family like I did.

The paradigm of having that "normal" family was haunting me terribly. It was what I grew up with. In my world, I always heard wise and mature women say that you have to suffer to keep the family together – that it's not about me; it's about my daughter. And I listened, until I made a decision to think differently. What if it's not true? How is keeping a family that, in reality, doesn't exist anymore, the right thing to do? What if my daughter doesn't have both her parents by her side all the time? What if she sees us separately, but both of us are happy? Wouldn't that be much more fair to her? She won't see the fights. She won't see me cry. She won't have a male role model performing this terrible type of behavior. I came to my senses and made a decision to act accordingly.

I have to admit, it was one of the best decisions I ever made. My daughter spends the best time with me and she spends time with him that is equally great. He tries to be a good father. He wasn't such a great husband, but she doesn't need a husband yet. Honestly, one thing I am very proud of is that I managed not to use her as a manipulative tool to get back at him. I never counted the time they spent together and tried to make an issue out of it like I know a lot of parents going through custody battles do. I don't mind if they go away on vacations or she stays at his house. I know how custody can get out of hand when a divorced mother gets a court order in her favor. I know it helps regulate the process, but it gets ridiculous because all the parties suffer in the end.

If you're afraid to make a decision, whether it's about getting out of a relationship, changing careers or starting to finally take care of your body and health, don't be. The wisest thing I came to realize is that in reality, you're not supposed to know how things are going to be or how it's going to work out for you; they just do. So please don't worry. Somehow, life opens the way once you make an important decision. It gives you the means to figure it out. It always does.

Making a few bold decisions was the start of my personal Wow. Amazing events begin to happen to you once you commit. "Make your decision!" Mr. Proctor's voice is always in my head. He makes it sound so convincing and powerful. Probably for the first time in my life, I allowed myself to make that decision based on nothing but a very big desire.

I used the same principle of making a decision based on my passionate desire to get myself into that bikini competition. Nowadays, a lot of women compete in fitness, so for some, such a step might be nothing special. The 40+ age group is respectfully called "Masters." To tell you the truth, by this age I was already a master in a few different areas, but definitely not in the best-looking body category.

My assets and credentials at that time (besides my greatest achievement: my daughter), were four university degrees. Faculty of Psychology at the University of Toronto, Faculty of Journalism at Moscow State University – PR and Advertising, Law Faculty at Moscow State University, and Law School at the University of Miami. I had two certifications in health and lifestyle coaching, was a certified fitness trainer, and a specialist in fitness nutrition. These are just the diplomas I remember, and have them in frames to prove it.

Photos of the new me fake-tanned and half-naked logically didn't fit in between those red stamped pieces of paper, proving an enormous investment of time and money. The bikini world, by the way, requires no less an investment. It was a fantasy field for me. It was like flying to the moon and back. It seemed nearly impossible. But it was possible, and it was done – and done again and again to prove that it wasn't random. That was Wow – Real Wow!! No, it was Wow Wow Wow!!

I revealed myself onstage in the sparkling Swarovski bikini, barely covering a far from ideal part of my body, which for a long time I was just sitting on physically and emotionally. It's a part that we're usually ashamed to unveil because of its imperfection. Yes, it was far from perfect – but that's my point. We're always waiting to be perfect before we start acting. How often did I not take action because I wanted to get just a little better beforehand? And then even better – get more education, more experience, become older and wiser and God knows what else. I wonder how much I've missed because of these protective measures that were keeping me from getting to the goal? This time I didn't wait to be perfect. Even after a few years of competing, I'm still very far from perfect, but a ton of amazing things have already happened. What if I'd waited for the right shape and look, the perfect time, or the ideal me? Logically, I didn't possess the tools to get there, but I knew my Wow factor, and based on that, the decision was made.

How do we usually make a decision? I thought I knew the proper way: we figure out all the pros and cons. We're taught to write them down in two separate columns and then weigh them to see what's going to work and what's not. In Russian, we have a saying: "Measure seven times and cut once." So, we measure and measure, we get more information, try it on, and then measure some more. Do we cut? No, because we're scared to make the wrong move.

Stop right there. How do you know what's going to work? Have you tried something like this before in your life? Probably not. Somebody else that's somewhat like you has tried and failed, or at least had this idea, but found it impossible to accomplish. So, her knowledge and experience become your own paradigm. You are now basing your decision on somebody else's experience. Does that make sense? What about the small percent of those who've succeeded? Why not focus on that? Why are you protecting yourself from the possibility of a positive outcome? Because your ego wants you to be safe, and you listen to it. I, on the other hand, invite you to try making a decision that's not based on logic, but on the Wow you've hopefully figured out by now.

This was the turning point, the beginning of miraculous changes in all spheres of my life. I felt like I'd received so many answers. Having read tons of books on personal development, I finally got to practice what I learned. It all came together and has changed my reality. It gave me a sense of inner freedom, and taught me many lessons on how things actually work and how to achieve something I really want. Perhaps most importantly, though, it relieved me from the fast-approaching fear of aging, the fear that I'm losing my vibrancy, my drive and my sex appeal. In reality, I've never experienced so much attention and energy from the opposite sex as I do now. From both sexes, actually. What an incredible relief to finally live without this fear! (Not that I'm 100 percent recovered, because I'm a woman, and our moods come and go). Still, it's amazing to feel ageless – at least, sometimes. Now I live in a somewhat different reality where I ask myself: what are you going to create next? What do you plan to achieve? I have no doubt that it's possible to do much more. I'm not so much striving to achieve as I am to simply be happy. My overwhelm is different now; it's that there are so many interesting things I want to try that are very much Wow. Which one to choose is the question. "So many men, so little time," as they say. Now I feel I have all the time in the world, but not too many men are Wow enough to be worth my time.

WOW WOMAN ACTION STEP 3

Are you ready to make a decision that resonates with your Wow?

Do this, please: Write down ALL the things you want to achieve, do, and try. Be careful here. Don't write the things you NEED to do; write down the things you WANT to do! Those that will let you feel the Wow you've already described for yourself, the ones that make you feel alive and happy, and the ones that bring you joy and content-ment. You know what they are because you've always wanted to do them, but you've been waiting until that perfect moment. Let's pretend this is the perfect moment. Just write it down.

You Were Born WOW!

_____

_____

_____

_____

_____

_____

_____

_____

_____

_____

_____

_____

_____

_____

_____

_____

_____

_____

_____

_____

_____

_____

_____

_____

Once again, the exercise is to write down. I know you are tempted to immediately put this idea to a rationality test and, most likely, based on your enormous experience and life expertise make a decision that it's not possible. I know you may want to cross it out a few times. I know, you'll be ashamed at yourself for having such outrageous ideas and bold plans. I know you will. And that's great. That means you're on the right track. But, I remind you, the point of this exercise is to write it down. That's it. Don't overdo the job, like you always do. Just let it be there on paper. Just leave it alone. And go do something interesting and exciting. Have a glass of wine, for example. Yes, it's okay to have wine. You have my permission as long as it's a good quality wine. Low in sugar, preferably. While sipping it, think about the fact that you were born Wow.

CHAPTER 4

Fake Your Enthusiasm, Not Your Orgasm

I was 22 when I went to Monaco for the first time. I was stunned by everything: the architecture, the history and overall greatness, the smell of wealth and prosperity, the sense of royalty. We all want to be princesses. We all want a prince, too. In Monaco, you actually feel like that fairytale can happen to you, because it happened to Grace Kelly. It happened to some others who moved there, too. If there's at least one success story, you can repeat it. And even if there's not a story, you can create one with perseverance and time.

The first time I happened to be in Monaco, I knew that one day I'd live there. When you're younger, you're much more adventurous and free. Why do we decide that we need to be restricted and responsible when we're grown? I don't know. It's too bad. We lose a lot by giving up that freedom and exchanging it for fake stability.

I had no means for a move, but the Law of Attraction did the job. I had a desire to live there, and the desire was strong and exciting. The decision was strong and, of course, written down. Unconsciously, I was sure the means would come.

It was a few years later when I proceeded with the action steps. Today, we have lots of courses on how to manifest, but at the time, there was no guide for moving to Monte Carlo without being wealthy or well-connected. But the Wow factor was so motivating, and then the means came. I met somebody who helped me open a bank account, which was a requirement to rent an apartment (not that I had the funds to cover even six months of rent). But I was sure that the basic French I'd studied earlier for some – at that time, unknown reason – would allow me to file for a work permit and find a job.

My next step to this day seems funny, even to me. As there were no apartments for rent where I wanted and could afford, the real estate agent asked me to wait until something came up. But me, the action-taker, felt like I couldn't just wait – I needed to take steps to get me closer to my goal. So I rented a car and travelled to the border city in Italy, Ventimiglia. The reason for going was that I needed to buy an iron and ironing board! I don't know why I imagined there were no irons in Monaco; I guess it was too royal for that housekeeping activity. I wanted to create my reality of Monaco being my home – and home, obviously, starts with an iron!

So I went to Ventimiglia and bought an iron. It gave me a great sense of accomplishment. I stayed in Monaco another couple of weeks and met a lot of interesting people. My new friend, Michael, who happened to be the doctor of the Prince, introduced me to the Prince himself.

"You have beautiful eyes," Albert told me. Who am I to argue with the Prince of Monaco? I also met other locals – Mr. Sean Connery, the best James Bond ever – and others who live at the Côte d'Azur during the fall and winter because it's unbelievably peaceful and quiet. They all escape in August: tourist invasion time.

I didn't succeed at finding an apartment in the two weeks I could afford to stay at the hotel, so I left my newly acquired belongings with my friend and went back to Russia to wait for an apartment to become available. I left physically, but mentally and emotionally I was still there, feeling myself in the position of somebody who already resides there. I was very passionate about it.

In Moscow, a friend invited me to his birthday party kind of last-minute. I didn't feel like going, but decided to go for an hour. As I walked in, one guy captured my attention. He was calm and looked content. He didn't jump around and wasn't drinking. The birthday boy introduced me. We started talking and I found out that he's a racecar driver. That's why he was calm; he needs to be. Otherwise, he might miss a turn. He offered me a ride home, and to my surprise, he drove so annoyingly slowly and carefully that I doubted his profession for a minute. Then he told me he was leaving in two days, and guess where he was going? Monaco, of course! He lives in Monaco. He even has his own iron. And now, as you already know, we have a daughter.

What else could this be if not the Law of Attraction in action? I visualized Monaco. I put myself in the role of someone who lives there. I did it passionately, often and with conviction, and my life in Monaco showed up. It had to; it's the law of the Universe.

We all have role models – people we want to look like or be like, or just have what they have. Usually, our thinking process is that we want what that somebody has. We want to possess her or his material wealth, knowledge, and experience. We think that if we do what she does and be like she is, then we'll have what she has. In reality, the mechanism is slightly different: very different, in fact. It's completely opposite. First you have to become the person you want to be. Then you start acting like that person, and then you get the results. You pretend to be Monégasque, you buy an ironing board, and – Voilà! – you get to be the Princess.

As women make plans to finally create the body of their dreams, to look fit, toned, sexy and attractive, we usually struggle with how to start and how to sustain our activity. By this time and age, we've learned countless theories on what to do and not a lot on how to do it. I felt an incredibly powerful sense of overwhelm. It was crushing to think that I was smart and educated, but wasn't seeing any results of that knowledge actually showing up on my body. I realized that I needed to think more thoroughly about the end goal. I felt like I was in an uncomfortable place, and even though I knew the actions I needed to take, I didn't really know where I was going. It's strange how we often try to get somewhere without even knowing where we are going.

One of the exercises that helped me, and that I recommend you try, is living as that new you. Try visualizing every aspect of the updated life you'll have. Imagine for yourself a position you want to be in, and then, with the help of awareness, consciously ask yourself: do I behave in accordance with this position, or do I deviate? For example: if you would like to be Queen of England, you should be asking yourself if you want to be a free woman who does what she wants, or if you want to be a queen, who is obliged to live and behave accordingly. Either one is okay, but then there's less disappointment if your man and others don't treat you like a queen. At least you'll have clarity on that and won't get upset.

Here's where we get to have fun! We can make reaching your goal a game, and we can call it the "Fake it 'til you make it!" game. Remember the desire you wrote down? Playfully, ask yourself how would that person behave? How would she think? What would she wear? What would her day be like?

That's what I did. When I made the decision to be an athlete of some sort, I had to start acting like one: pretend, fake, make. Needless to say, faking was against my beliefs, but a game is a game. You are allowed. So, as I was doing that hated cardio every morning for an hour, I'd pretend to be a real athlete. I know a lot of athletes. I'm friends with and have worked with some top tennis players, hockey players and Olympic athletes. During those long cardio hours, I'd often wonder, "Would she – the real athlete – allow herself to make a decision to stop before the 60th minute? Would she be telling herself, 'I am very tired, my legs are hurting, I didn't get enough sleep, I don't have time', etc.?" These thoughts made me smile – and also made me go on.

I had a client in my private coaching program, this beautiful, bright woman who was substantially overweight. It felt like she was carrying all of her extensive respon-sibilities around her waist. In a way, it was a protective lifeline. It was her way of defending herself against the outside world, and she was carrying the weight of her duties on her body. We figured out that she wanted to feel better. She wanted to breathe easier and walk lighter, so we created a new role for her. She became a butterfly.

(No, we didn't dress her up with wings. We left that for Halloween). Rather, she started to act as if she was a butterfly. She tried to walk differently, spoke softer and moved lighter. Her physical behavior changed, and so has her whole self. She didn't lose too much weight, but became comfortable in her own skin and felt like the goal was achieved. She became a butterfly, and people love butterflies. They started reacting differently to her; they started to notice her inner beauty.

WOW WOMAN ACTION STEP 4

Based on your previous answers – create your role. Who or what do you want to be like?

_____

_____

_____

_____

_____

_____

_____

_____

_____

_____

_____

_____

_____

_____

Describe this persona. What's her day like?

_____

_____

_____

_____

_____

_____

_____

Who's in her social circle?

_____

_____

_____

_____

_____

_____

Where does she live?

_____

_____

_____

_____

_____

_____

What does she eat?

_____

_____

_____

_____

_____

_____

Where does she go?

_____

_____

_____

_____

_____

_____

What type of work does she do?

_____

_____

_____

_____

_____

_____

What does she do for fun?

_____

_____

_____

_____

_____

_____

What makes her happy?

_____

_____

_____

_____

_____

_____

What's important to her?

_____

_____

_____

_____

_____

_____

Try it on! Try being her. Come on, it's fun! Really. For once, be an actress. Imagine, be and act.

You'll get a feel for what you like about that new you. You'll understand what you don't accept, and what works or doesn't work for you personally.

Come on, enjoy it! This is probably the only time I will allow fakeness into a Wow woman's life.

Fake it, fake it, and fake it. Fake being Wow, and you will soon feel with every part of you that you were really born Wow, and nothing has changed since.

CHAPTER 5

Clarity is the New Self-charity

earned my first law degree from Moscow State University. I had my three-year-old daughter in my hands and I had just left her father and taken nothing with me. Why I wanted to be a lawyer is still an enigma to me. I don't like documents, I hate desk and research work, and I detest routine. I guess I loved the visual, the outside picture of it. I was visualizing myself sharply dressed, looking incredibly sexy (and at the same time, professional), meeting with clients and helping them solve their major life problems. As far back as I remember, I always wanted to help people. That's why I originally got a degree in psychology, back in the '90s. As a psychologist, I thought I'd help a lot of struggling people. I was quite disappointed that, besides different theories, I hadn't found too much practical use for psychology. Now I understand that what I actually wanted "to do was help people reach their goals without going back into their past, without questioning the root of the problem, and without the couch. (Okay, we can keep the couch). I just wanted to help them get from where they are now to where they ideally want to be. Little did I know, it's called coaching. It only took me 20 years of research to figure that out. I told you: research is not my forte.

When I was in that law school in Russia, I had already had the experience of living in Canada and the States. I remember gathering my fellow classmates and telling them of all the beautiful features of the foreign judicial system – of people's rights and the presumption of innocence. They loved my motivational speeches. I opened their eyes to a different world, and one day, I had my eyes opened.

On one of the school breaks I went to Miami. I love Miami. I love it so much that it could even be the real reason I went through another law school and got a Master's degree in international law from the University of Miami. I just wanted to be there. If not for love, then I don't understand how I could have invested so much time and effort in that very difficult education. For months, I lived 100 meters from the ocean and didn't go to the beach. I couldn't spend enough time with my daughter and I basically didn't have a life for a long time. I think it was probably an ego thing. I knew that doctors and lawyers are two of the most respected professions, so I definitely needed to be one of them. I guess it was that need for respect I was looking for, and not countless billed hours. Ironically, a lot of what I do now as a health and life coach is somewhat like being a doctor.

Before law school, I often visited Miami for fun. That vacation was like any other from my lifestyle then: beach during the day; restaurants and clubs at night. We went to a hip place and sat at a VIP table, champagne a tout le monde. Just the way we like it – the Wow style. I was sitting on the back of the couch observing the dancers and watching the club scene. VIP tables are usually well protected from the "normal" people. Of course, you are abnormal when you pay $5000 for a table with a couple of bottles of champagne and vodka. Oh! They also give you cranberry juice and throw in some strawberries to help you justify your stupid ego investment.

Out of the blue, this unknown girl comes straight to the table and starts pouring herself a drink. I'm okay with that. I'm just watching. First of all, I'm not paying for it – my friends are. And secondly, it's normal club scene practice. What's not normal is that she freely sits on my YSL jacket. I ask her, nicely, to find another place to sit. She's not too happy about it, but disappears. The next time I see her, she's talking to my friend, a good-looking guy. He's actually a hockey player. (This thing with me and hockey players is the story of my life, but that's another book). I'm fine with that since I don't pretend to be more than friends with the guy. I'm actually happy for them. Next time I see her is when I start to feel some liquid pouring over me. I quickly turn and see her next to me, turning away. WTF? My first reaction is to hit her right in her beautiful face, but I remember that I'm a lady – that I am Wow. Wow women fight gracefully, so I take my glass of champagne and slowly, with class, pour it over her head.

She turns to me, and something happens fast. I feel glass all over my hands and face. To this day, I don't know what happened. Either the glass broke in my hands, or she tried to cover her face and the ring on my finger hit the glass. In any case, it shattered into hundreds of little tiny pieces, and I had a ton of little bleeding cuts. She disappeared, and my friends gave me vodka to put on the wounds. There was no fight; I didn't even get up off the couch! It was an attack I didn't expect. The manager came to the table and asked me to step out to the office. I assured him it was okay and that I didn't have a problem. "We do," he replied, and told me again to step out.

Up until that moment, I was still expecting an apology, and at the very least, some more free strawberries. God, was I wrong! I saw a fire truck and a police car, and people gathered, looking to be entertained while they were waiting to get into the best club on Miami Beach. I didn't know I was the star of their night, that they were waiting for me. Me – the criminal, the aggressor.

I heard somebody screaming, "You're going to jail!" I realized it was the girl, getting out of the fire truck with her hand wrapped in a bandage. I was being called into the truck next.

As I'm showing my little cuts to the doctor, trying to find support to prove I was attacked, the young doctor/ fireman (looking like he stepped out of a firemen calendar) says, "Katia, sit down. I know she's full of shit. But, be prepared: you are going to jail. Call me when you get out. I'll help you figure it out." What he meant is that she cut herself to press charges and get some money out of me. It turned out to be a normal practice on Miami Beach.

A small but aggressive policewoman asked me to put my hands behind my back and handcuffed me. I'd watched American movies before, and I knew she was supposed to read me my Miranda rights. You know: "You have the right to remain silent. Anything you say can and will be used against you in a court of law…"

I asked her about that, and boom! She hit me from behind and pushed me right into the trunk of the car. I don't want to describe all the nice things I was told and had done to me in the police department. I'll just describe the feelings: humiliation and disrespect. Nasty comments were made by the policeman, almost lying in his chair with his feet on the table.

Another officer came in with the report. "She took a glass, broke it at the bar and stabbed the girl," the officer said.

What bar? There was no bar anywhere near me. I didn't even get up off the couch. I didn't do anything! I felt like crying out of despair, but who cared?

They put me in a truck and closed the door. I was lucky that the policeman who took me to the car was kind enough to change my handcuffs from the real ones to the lighter version, like the ones from a sex shop. I managed to get one arm out of them. At least I got some movement back.

It was freezing and dark in there. The two metal benches were too cold to sit on. You know the philosophical idea that we have everything we need in life within arm's reach? It's true! We have everything we need to achieve our goals; we just choose not to see those tools. My goal at that particular moment was to lie down on something warm, and the tool was there. The desire to look a little sexier and more attractive is on every woman's mind. At the time, I'd lost some weight and it was great – but when you lose fat, you know what else is lost? Your lingerie size. But we have our little secrets. And we have silicone pads. Shhhh. Don't tell men. They don't like to be deceived. Let's keep it our secret. This time, as there were no men around, I took the silicone pads out of my bra and used them to keep my head off the cold bench. It was such a relief already.

I don't know how long I was there. Nobody answered my screaming that I needed to go to the bathroom. Sorry for the details, but I have to mention that I was forced to use the floor of the truck to pee. Quite an experience. In a couple of hours, I assume, I saw through a little hole in the back of the truck that some more people were being brought to the truck. These, I could tell, were the worst ones: the Miami Beach drug addicts. Luckily, they were all men, so they were placed on the other side of the truck. We started moving.

Any movement is better than stagnation. The worst thing is nothing happening. That's one of the lessons of this incident.

And then the real movie began. We arrived somewhere. Through the little window, I could just make out a metal fence slowly opening up. *Jail*, I think. *Okay. It will be over soon. Now I'll call a lawyer and they'll let me out on bail.*

As I walked in, three big mamas were welcoming me into my new world. "Are you suicidal?"

"No."

"Red carpet. Front, side pose for pictures. Shoes off. Ohhh, Manolo Blahnik?"

One of the guards held up my black, five-inch sexy heels and started screaming, "Manolo! Manolo!" (Yes, *Sex and the City* was popular at the time). They met their Bradshaw: I met my hell.

As we approached the female part of the jail, I saw two cells – one with 30+ women, and another with three or four. From what I understood, they were the dangerous ones. The guards left me in the corridor. "You can make a couple of phone calls," they told me. "And your bail is $7,000."

"No problem," I said, feeling like the hell was almost over. "I can pay right away, if you give me back my crocodile

Gucci bag." They had taken all my belongings to storage – my Manolos, my bag, my jacket and cash – and replaced them with rubber slippers in exchange.

Not so fast. They don't accept credit cards; somebody has to bring cash. It's the United States. Nobody has that much cash on them. And it's Sunday. So, I call my mother. "Please sit down," I tell her. "I'm okay, but I'm in jail. Please find $7,000, and take care of my daughter." I don't know what my mom went through at this moment. It must've been tough to find out that your daughter is in jail for stabbing somebody.

They left me in the corridor. I thought they'd see I didn't belong there, that I'd be spared the indignity of being locked up. Yeah, right. "Barbie, get in."

As I entered the cell with more than 30 alleged criminals, there were only two benches that sat 15. Here, I learned another lesson, this one about the position you take to serve your needs. I realized that if I didn't sit down, I'd be on a cold floor, with filth and worse. I'd spare you the details, but then my story wouldn't be complete. There was vomit and urine on the floor. I decided to fit in.

"Move," I said loudly to the girls sitting on the side of the bench. The leader of the tribe, this woman who thought she was a gangsta man, wowed me with respect. Taking the right position always works: I got my seat.

Gangsta woman started talking to me. "Hey you, wassup? Where you from, honey? Nice boobs. Are they real, or did you pay the big bucks, Blondie?"

Remember that my goal was to fit in, not to follow my morals or fight for my rights. I needed to gain authority and be accepted. Now, for the second time, the silicone pads helped me. I made a show of taking them out of my bra and passed them over to her.

"Here, have them. Have your new boobs. Enjoy," the whole cell burst out with laughter and acceptance.

The guards called me Barbie. They also called me Kournikova. Remember the Russian tennis player who was more celebrated for her looks than her game? She starred in what I considered to be a phenomenal commercial for the sports bra. The slogan was, "Only the ball should bounce!" You see her looking awesome, jumping up and down. I guess they found some resemblance to Anna Kournikova, even though I was not jumping. I was rather still, as I'd lost most of my energy by then. The guards were having fun: I was not. I was waiting to be bailed out. Hours went by. People were coming and going, and still, I sat there. One of the things I had to get used to was going to the bathroom. There were two toilets. I wasn't accustomed to doing these things in public, but you can get used to it. The other thing that was really hard to accept is that I was there for doing nothing.

The scariest thing was that my brain was giving up on me. After hours of no sleep and stress, it had started to imagine crazy things. *What if it really happened? What if I did stab somebody? What if I spend the next 10 years in prison?* Your brain and your thoughts can be your best friends, but they can also be your worst enemies. Never believe the thoughts you are thinking. They are not reality; they are not you.

As you can see, I had no idea and no clarity on what would happen next. There was no plan, because I had no control over the situation. It's so important to gain as much clarity as possible in anything you want to achieve.

To make this long, 15-hour ordeal short, my friends brought the money. It was the end of the day when I got released. Actually, they brought the money at 11 in the morning, but the system does this on purpose to make things hard. They want you to experience this torture so you don't want to come back. Ever since then, I call security when somebody is jeopardizing my well-being. Believe me, this system works well: you don't ever want to come back.

After I got out and contacted a lawyer, I spent another $7,000 getting myself out of it. Obviously, the charges were dropped. They had cameras at the club, and I didn't do anything. But I did learn some lessons, and I'm quite certain I needed those lessons. It cooled down my hot-blooded Russian temper. I started being more careful and appreciative of life and freedom – freedom to have clarity, to be in control, to choose and regulate my emotions. I'll never respond to an attack with even the slightest move. I understand now that the presumption of innocence works a bit differently than I thought. Whoever calls the police first is right until proven otherwise. I am SO grateful for that lesson.

The reason this prison incident happened in the first place is because a lot of women, like me, think and act based on our emotions. In contrast to most men, we use our right half of the brain, which is emotional. Men use the logical left half. I came to the conclusion that it would be very beneficial if we could change that and learn to choose our emotions and act smart, like our men do.

Before eliciting any emotion, there's a fraction of time that passes between the thought and your reaction to it. At that moment, we all have a choice of which emotion to choose. (Yes, there is enough time. We can test it).

Let's pretend you're driving down the road in your convertible in Santa Monica. The sun is shining, the music is great. You're happy. All of a sudden, this sports car cuts you off and puts on the blinkers to apologize. You're not too happy about it. He destroyed your peaceful Sunday afternoon. You want revenge.

As you press on the gas pedal and get close to that enemy of yours, you're ready to explode. Then you see that the driver is Brad Pitt. What would you do? What emotion would you choose? Most likely, you'd smile, and your whole day (or next days or weeks) would be different. That day would've been different if you had chosen a different emotion –if it wasn't Brad and you'd given him the finger.

Usually, men don't really understand us. "Honey, did I gain weight? Do I look fat?" You're not really asking for the truth. You're waiting for him to assure you that you're the most beautiful woman on the planet. But he honestly (and you want him to always be honest with you, don't you?) tells you the truth. "Yes, you did gain some weight." And most likely, he'll advise you to stop eating. "Just stop eating," he tells you, "and you'll lose it." Plain and simple.

Of course it's simple. And it's logical. But we don't think logically; we think emotionally. We have a relationship with food: a love/hate relationship. We love it, we hate it, and we feel guilty about it. We use it to relieve boredom. We need it for our self-esteem. We get attached. We're obsessed. We break up. We reconcile. Any type of emotion, as long as we're not indifferent.

By the way, we often think hate is the opposite of love, but it's actually just the other side of love. It's the same feeling, but flipped. Indifference is the opposite. As long as there's an emotion being directed at us, that means there's caring going on. I was just explaining it to my daughter, who's 14.

She's a professional ballroom dancer. She has danced and competed from early childhood. She wants to be on stage. She wants to be famous. I never allowed that thought for myself. I was told it's vain, and vanity is not respected in society. Neither was taking care of oneself more than others. It would be considered selfish and egotistic. But in reality, through fame, you can give something positive and valuable to those who need your energy or knowledge. Like this book, for example. I'm sharing something valuable I have to share.

I'm helping my daughter admit to herself that she wants fame, and it's okay to want that. I help her understand she'll be faced with a lot of hate – hate that is actually love. As long as there is an emotion towards you, you are good. Bad publicity is still publicity, as we all know.

Back to our emotions and food. If we take a man's approach, we just choose our goal, come up with steps, and act. *But what do I do with my emotions?* you ask. *I have emotions. I have hormones, too. And by the way, they get out of whack by the time we are 40. I'm a woman, after all.*

First, try attaching your emotions not to the process, but to the result you get. For example, I get asked all the time how I handle an hour of cardio. Isn't it hard? Isn't it boring? It is. It was in the beginning. I counted every minute, looking at my watch constantly. Time is really slow when you're waiting and very fast if you're late. While passionately waiting for it to end, you're going through a range of emotions like pain, denial, regret, despair and happiness. You spend your cardio moments emotionalizing your present life, but then you learn to accept it as it is. You accept the fact that cardio is just something that your body and mind are doing in the moment; it's not who you are. You're not a bunch of drawn in, contradicting emotions. And then you willingly focus on the outcome. What will this "suffering" bring me? Remember your Wow factor? Remember your why? If that Why is strong enough and your happiness is at the other end of the treadmill work-out, won't you give it all you've got during those (now seemingly much shorter) 60 minutes? Of course you will.

And then, just like a man, you learn to choose your emotions according to your goal. Practice it by bringing awareness to that fraction of a second when the choice is about to be made. Ask yourself the question: is this reaction getting me closer to my goal, or away from it? You'll always get an honest answer. Then you most likely won't react and lose control of the situation. Instead, you'll act and get what you want. Like everything else, this takes practice.

Maybe the first hundred times, you'll be reacting out of habit, but on the hundred and first try, you'll finally master it. And believe me, you won't be a victim of your emotions; you'll be in control. This is a really satisfying feeling! Unless, in reality, you don't want to be in control. Maybe you're using your victimhood to get something else: care, support, sympathy. If that's the case, then don't complain that you're not achieving your dreams. In reality, you don't want change – you just want attention. You won't get much from me, because that's not about being Wow. Wow women propel through the fear of the uncom-fortable unknown. A Wow woman is in control. And she is at ease at the same time, because she trusts the process called life.

As we choose our emotions, we choose everything else in life. What we have now are the results of previous choices. Some of them work well for us, and some don't. We may not even remember when and where we made that choice. At the time, it was the best decision according to the circumstances. After making that choice, we built the rest of our life around it, thinking it was the right thing to do. It becomes a habit, a paradigm. We feel like it's the real us. Maybe we were born with it. Maybe it's Maybelline – but it's not the real you. It's a habit, a mechanical repetition of the same behavior without conscious thinking, without awareness. If you want to change the habit, you absolutely must bring back the awareness to making new choices in alignment with the new circumstances. It's a skill, like building muscles. But it's a great skill. Master it.

WOW WOMAN ACTION STEP 5

Once you have clarity on what you want, you need to do one last little thing: take action. A lot of us struggle with being persistent and persevering to reach the goal. We tend to change our minds and renegotiate our scheduled tasks with ourselves. We slip on the rocky road. Sticking to the plan and keeping the performance is hard. We all know that. But how often do you slip if you've signed a contract with somebody? You're bound to perform your obligations, or you may incur fees or other unpleasant outcomes.

I didn't go to law school for nothing, you know. I learned that contracts work quite well with people. This is why I'm offering you one to sign with yourself to keep you accountable.

Yes, you are the competent party. The subject matter is you delivering the service of doing the best for yourself and achieving your goals. You'll have a "meeting of the mind" with yourself, where you agree to have your rights and to perform your duties. In case of a breach of contract, your damages will be your own losses of not having a new and improved joyful life.

Please fill this out.

I, _____ (name)

am _____

(choose five qualities from the exercise in Chapter One that resonate with you the most. (for example – I AM: loving, caring, sexy, bold and beautiful) and state them as if you already possess these qualities).

_____

_____

_____

_____

_____

_____

_____

_____

_____

_____

_____

_____

_____

_____

_____

_____

_____

_____

As I am now obligated to perform my contractual duties, I promise to act according to these qualities of a Wow woman for as long as it takes me to become one.

In case of non-performance, I will live with regret, feeling unfulfilled and unsatisfied.

Sign it. Date it. Print it out on a large piece of paper. Color it to give it life and vibrancy.

In reality, if you love yourself, and if you feel like your word is important and worth something, this won't be a very difficult task for you to perform. Learn to value your word and your promises – especially the ones you make to yourself.

You have entered into a contract with somebody you respect and adore, with somebody who was born Wow – with you!

CHAPTER 6

Do You Want to Be Perfect? Or Would You Rather Be Wow?

My own journey of finding a Wow woman to emulate started around age 14 – exactly how old my daughter is now. I remember when I began to realize that, as a woman, I needed to take care of myself in all different aspects. I started using make-up, buying creams, and performing self-made manicures that ended up in blood and wounds. I experimented with my mother's clothes. In fact, when my parents went away on weekends, half of my class experimented with her clothes. We also did some chemistry lessons with my father's liquor to figure out how much water to add to whiskey so that nobody notices.

The notion of being skinny and the awareness of calories and diets came into my life through some western magazines that slowly started to be available after the Moscow Olympic Games in 1980. I started counting calories and writing them in a special journal. I tried fasting for days and used some anorexia and bulimia techniques.

Why was I doing it? At 14, a girl is starting to become a Wow woman. She's looking for her new identity. She's trying on different versions of herself. She feels grown up, but lacks experience. She needs support, but feels like her parents just don't get it. Parents do get it – they just forget that they were exactly the same. As a mother of a teenager, I try not to forget. I attempt to remember how it felt to be criticized and judged. I felt torn between what I had started to experience myself and what my parents were telling me because they "knew better."

My loving and caring father knew that he knew better and once said in front of some people that I'd gained weight. If you're a dad, never say that in front of people. It hurts – badly. It may become a life-long wound that will never heal.

Us women were born high achievers as much as we were born Wow. I'm certainly one. I like to achieve more and more. Society accepts it as a respectable thing. It's good to have high goals and it's good to strive for more and more. What's not as widely accepted is the idea that to be happy, you don't have to achieve more. You don't have to have more. Instead, you need to have achieved enough and feel like you have enough. The notion of being and having enough is so simple, yet so difficult to get a hold of. It simply means appreciating what you have.

I know exactly where my own feeling of not being enough came from, and most likely, you do too. For me, it came from my father. He was a very loving human being, but had high standards for himself and those he loved. My dad was a high achiever. He was rather successful, even during the toughest communist times. He had connections. He knew a lot of people from the government, to the mafia, to the police, to the celebrities. These people trusted him. In the jewelry business, you have to be trustworthy. Actually, in every business you must be trustworthy – but in diamonds, especially.

In the '90s, he had a store on the famous Arbat Street. I grew up seeing renowned people coming to him on different occasions – in good times to buy gifts, and in bad times to sell their stones and watches.

I still have one of those stones. It's a one-carat diamond from Galina, the daughter of Leonid Brezhnev. She was recognized for loving precious stones. She had the greatest collection of them all. My father also kept the setting of that ring. It looks like a flower with five petals. Each petal is a one-carat diamond. My father kept one carat for me and sold the other four. I wanted to fill that setting with new diamonds, but Ms. Brezhnev's fingers were so big that it was impossible to size the ring for me without damaging it. So now I just keep it as a childhood memory.

My father always wanted me to achieve more. Sometimes I think that he created an ideal image of a Wow woman in his head and wanted me to become one. Not having any feminine role model (his mother passed away when he was 13), he had to invent one. He took me to every possible activity from figure skating to volleyball to piano lessons and choir, so I could become better and better. I hated the piano teacher. This older woman asked my father not to bring me back, as I was not behaving the proper way (whatever that meant). I could actually sing pretty well. My second alto was a rare thing, so I was chosen by the music professor to have private lessons with the vocal coach. I was 12 and didn't understand why I felt so uncomfortable with that male teacher. He was buttering me up with compliments and touching my body with his sweaty hands. Later, I realized that he could have been a pedophile. Thankfully, nothing happened, but I quit, because I felt he wanted more from me than just hitting those high notes.

My whole childhood, I received mixed feelings from my parents, especially my father. On the one hand, I was the best daughter – loved and a source of pride. On the other, no matter what new skills I acquired or what grades I achieved, I only got, "Okay, nice, but you can do more."

This "but" always stood between me and my happiness. Up to this day the "but" is haunting me, and it's most likely haunting you in your pursuit of happiness and satisfaction. It can be your mother, teacher, older brother or anyone else who was your role model and wanted you to grow, who wished you the best. But the strongest message we remember, the lesson we've all learned, is that we are not enough – and we go through life with that "but" in our heads.

Oftentimes it does help to achieve, but other times it distresses and disappoints. In any case, this "BUT" is not going anywhere. I think the best we can do for ourselves is to try to accept it. Accept the fact that our parents didn't know any better. They didn't take any motivational seminars on how to be a role model. They didn't read any self-help books on parenting. Most likely, that's how they were brought up. That's how their parents motivated them. Recognize that it's not you who's not enough; it's them who never got enough.

For many years I continued trying different ways of being the perfect me. So do a lot of women, especially high achievers, who are on the constant search for perfection. When I was around 20, I had a friend whose mother was 45, as I am now. She was a good-looking, very kind and loving woman. No matter how good-looking or loving you are, though, some men still need to have social proof that they're still a young, wild stud. So, they find somebody to help them get that feeling back.

My friend's mom discovered her husband had found a woman to express his enormous sexuality with. There wasn't much she could do to stop him, but as a Wow woman, she could do something for herself. She decided to improve – to become young, sexy and perfect again. She became a vegetarian. Then she became vegan, and then a raw food enthusiast. I remember her making juices out of everything green. She quit eating salt. She told me, "Katia, the food is talking to me. It tells me what's good and what's evil for me. We have a great relationship."

Obviously, her body was protesting. It refused to function. It stopped digestion totally. Then her mind started to give up. When her husband took her to the hospital, she took it as an insult. She claimed he wanted to commit her and get rid of her.

One day I was pulling up to their building and saw the police and an ambulance. I also saw a covered body on the ground. There was blood. As I got to the apartment, there was an investigation going on. She had jumped out of the twelfth floor window. As the police finished their agenda, I was the first one to walk into the room. I'll never forget what I saw: a neatly laid out pair of black pants on the bed and a white button-down silk shirt. A pair of black high heels were standing on the floor beside the bed. She'd prepared her clothes to look perfect in the coffin.

This terrible event changed a lot of things in my life. For about six months, I couldn't study, couldn't function properly. It made me think a lot and reevaluate ideas about the search for perfection, diets and self-worth. It made me suffer a lot, but it helped me grow even more. I realized that first, perfection is unreachable, and second, not needed. Happiness doesn't mean being perfect – it's being enough as you are. Of course, you can do more, but only if it brings you joy.

You want to take action to improve yourself when you love yourself and desire to be even better. Many women hate their looks and their bodies, and try to improve them. This position doesn't get them far. First, learn to love and accept yourself. Then act. Take imperfect action steps, and you'll see results.

It's easy to say, "Love yourself." How do I start loving myself? Do I wake up one day and realize, *Oh! All of a sudden I'm loving myself!* Actually, yes – but not because it just happens. You make a decision and continuously focus on the positive side of you: "I love myself. I accept myself. I love my flaws. I know my great attributes." In a while, you start believing yourself and actually see the best parts of you. It's just a habit of focusing on the good – a great habit! Again, it's like building a muscle: the "loving yourself" muscle.

WOW WOMAN ACTION STEP 6

How often do you talk to yourself?

Not those doubts in your mind, or the discussions that don't let you sleep at night. Not those decision-making processes of whether you should get that dress or pass on it. I mean a real eye-to-eye conversation with yourself. I've had this type of conversation with myself for years. Actually, it wasn't really a dialogue; it was a monologue. *I don't like my glutes*, I was saying to myself for years. One day, I decided to accept it. Once I removed the emotional part of not accepting it, the logical side of me did the job. That part made me do the work, without having that old monologue. For months, I worked on that part of my body. In the beginning, I saw very little improvement. I was devastated and ready to give up. *I'm too old for this. It will never happen to me. What a waste of time and energy…*

Then one day, an old friend that I hadn't seen for a while who was unaware of my new lifestyle asked me where I got my glutes done. I proudly announced the name of the gym and the trainer helping me. She looked at me and asked how. She was shocked, since she was sure I had butt implants. Imagine how focusing on the good and persistence can save you tons of money on surgeries!

Decide to love yourself as you are. I'm sure there are things you love about yourself. List them.

Write them down. Read them aloud to yourself daily.

_____

_____

_____

_____

_____

_____

_____

_____

_____

_____

_____

_____

_____

_____

_____

_____

_____

_____

_____

_____

Stand in front of a mirror. Look yourself in the eye. For 10, 20, 30 seconds. Maybe more, maybe less, until you almost get uncomfortable. It's a weird feeling, I know. I cried the first few times.

Keep looking, explore your face. Do you like what you see? Do you like who you see? Who is that woman looking at you? Is she happy? Is she satisfied? How do you feel?

_____

_____

_____

_____

_____

_____

_____

_____

_____

_____

_____

_____

_____

_____

_____

_____

_____

_____

Tell your reflection you love her. Keep telling her how much you adore her, how much you appreciate everything she's done for you. Tell her that she's a Wow woman. Tell her that you loved her from the moment she was born.

Make a pact with yourself to love yourself as you are in this moment. With all your flaws and imperfections. If you don't like your thighs, just accept that fact. And then think about all the things your thighs do for you without you even thinking about it: they carry you everywhere you need to go, they support you continuously, they're there for dancing and feeling joyful; running, walking, bowling – whatever makes you feel good.

Enjoy your thighs, make a decision to love them. And only then think of a plan to improve them because we can make things better only when we love being with the things we were born with. For some reason, we're used to thinking differently – we start from a position of hatred and then try to fix or change things. No, the mechanism is different. What do you love about your thighs or whatever body part(s) you'd like to transform?

_____

_____

_____

_____

_____

_____

_____

_____

_____

_____

_____

When you act from a position of love, one day you'll wake up and love them. Once you change this habit and add action to it, you'll be operating as if you were born Wow. And we both know you were…

CHAPTER 7

Wrong Actions, Right Outcomes

A ll this meditation is good, you tell me, but what do I have to do to achieve my goal? What do I do next? What are my action steps? How do I choose these steps? How do I know they're the right kind of steps? Our men are going to help us, as they often do. We can put aside our emotions and feelings. (Not that men don't have feelings). Of course they do. But those successful, high achievers we look up to use logic for their action process. Then we write out the plan. The number one mistake we make is trying to create the perfect plan that will work flawlessly. Accept the fact that it will never happen! Your plan will change and evolve. Just as you are allowed to try on 20 pairs of jeans until they finally fit you more or less okay, it's alright to try different ways of getting to your goal and the results you want. You'll have to tweak the plan to do this, and that's okay.

The desired result we want to achieve is created in our minds. Sometimes we overestimate our end result, so if we come up even a little short, we feel like we've failed. If I want to be 127 pounds, then 128.5 doesn't work. If I don't get to 127, then I'm not an achiever. If we divorce after a 20-year marriage, we call it a "failed marriage." I could never understand that, honestly. What about those 10.5, or even two years of my life, that were happy? What about those times when we had fun and were loving? What about our beautiful children? I refuse to call that a failed marriage. That was a very successful marriage that simply ended. In the same way, it's okay to change your plan. What worked in the past needs to be tweaked and changed as you continue to grow, just like a marriage or any other partnership. The partnership between you and your body changes and grows with time.

Think about me participating in a contest that was totally out of my league. That seemed impossible until I did it. Then I achieved it for three more years in a row just to be sure it wasn't a fluke. Could I ever have imagined receiving a jacket from my physical fitness association before going to the Nationals with the words "National Athlete" on my back? Who? Me? Is this real? A national athlete? Is that a good result or a great result?

I was in tears when I put it on. *What kind of national level athlete am I? I'm 44. I'm a lawyer. I don't belong here.* But I still have the jacket to prove my thoughts wrong.

One other thing that bothers me a lot is when people ask me if I won. Did you get first place? A gold medal? Honestly, this is very irritating. The process of winning the gold takes a little more dedication, commitment and time – if that's the goal, of course. That wasn't my goal. My goal was to get there, to go up on that stage and not to drop dead right there. Or worse – run from the stage, crying. And, as a little bonus, instead of a gold medal, I got some other trophies – like the body of my dreams and the self-confidence to go with it. Not many understand that, though. They still want the gold and feel miserable when they get silver.

A few years ago, it was almost scientifically proven that other shades of grey exist – at least 50 of them. So, your results aren't exactly black and white. They can be different, depending on how the light of your brain falls on it. I chose for my golden grey to be bright and shining. I chose to value and treasure my not-so-perfect actions and not-so-gold results.

Many women have major difficulties with taking action when it comes to working on their bodies and health. We're fed so much information with so many different theories, ideas and meal plans. We don't know who we should listen to or trust. We're trying to find the one and only plan that will get us to our goal, but feelings of overwhelm and anxiety freeze our bodies. We're afraid to take action and do the wrong thing. We're afraid we won't get results and will have gone through all that effort for nothing.

After my law school graduation, I took the Bar exam in New York State (one of the most difficult bar exams, by the way). I'll spare you the details of the preparation process, but it was tough. Studies say that if you don't spend six hours per day studying on the weekdays and four hours on the weekends for three months before the exam, your chances of passing are slim to none. I didn't. I spent less. I was already a 38-year-old single mother of a first grader. I was not as committed as the 22-year-olds whose whole life depended on the exam.

Taking the exam was one of the most stressful events in my life. Just that exam alone justifies why lawyers make so much money. They're warriors. They fight. They aren't called sharks for nothing. Maybe I didn't want to be a shark, or I just didn't study enough, but I was short a few points. I didn't pass. Of course, my perfect plan was taking it again, but I never did.

I got criticized a lot for that. A lot of people looked at it as a failure, but my idea of failure is doing something you don't want to do. I think failure is getting up and having to go do work that you're not passionate about and that doesn't bring you joy every day.

Honestly, I was in love with the vain idea of being a lawyer, and not with the everyday practice of being one. I was serving my ego more than my real needs. My ego got satisfied the minute I got my diploma. As I was sitting at the graduation ceremony at the University of Miami, I remember one of the speakers saying, "Do you understand that you belong to a very small group of people that have reached this level of education?" That was enough for me. My ego investment paid off right then and there.

Not passing the New York Bar was one of the best things that ever happened to me. Of course, as a "normal" striving-for-perfection goal achiever, I was very disappointed. When I got my results, I was participating in a Tony Robbins training event. I had the coal-walking exercise that day. Being in that environment helped a little. I felt empowered and ready to take the Bar exam again six months later.

As I was preparing for the second try, my best friend called. "Haven't you had enough of studying? Why don't you come and practice everything you've learned? Let's see if you pass the Bar of my standards."

I love challenges, and he knew it. To take the position, I'd have to move to Moscow and run a construction project.

I took it and started running the project, doing some legal, management and organizational work. I enjoyed doing it, admired the people I worked with, and enjoyed the atmosphere. I absolutely loved getting up in the mornings, getting ready, putting on a nice suit and heels, and going to the office. (Mind you, the office was at the Ritz-Carlton Hotel, Moscow. That might have helped, too). As you can imagine, going back to study for a Bar exam was out of the question.

But the project was soon over. We completed it success-fully, and it was time to move on. All of a sudden, I had some free time on my hands. I had to temporarily fill it with activities, so I made a decision to dedicate this time to my body and mind. I hired a trainer and started exercising three to four times a week. As an information junkie, I was asking lots of questions about nutrition and exercise. I was fascinated by how much new information I was learning, but it wasn't enough. The more I found out, the more lost I felt. I felt like the trainer was not giving away the knowl-edge he possessed. He wanted me to attend more and more sessions and spend more money. My sessions were three to six times a week, so I was spending a lot. Since I still didn't have clarity, I decided to learn for myself. I got certified as a personal trainer and fitness nutrition specialist, and also became a health coach and integrative nutrition coach. After law school I promised myself I'd never study again, so I lied. You can even sue me.

Another crucial mistake we make when creating a plan? We think way too big! It's good to think big, but it's often so overwhelming that we get stuck. We overcomplicate things because we think we're here to save the world – and that is so big and challenging that it may become impossible. This is always my biggest challenge. I see the big picture and dream big, but then I freeze. Now, I do some reverse engineering to get out of that conditioning. I dissect the process into microscopic, imperfect actions. When we create miniature steps, they're easily doable. Want to run a marathon? Don't study the theory of how to decrease your running time by five percent – just buy running shoes, for God's sake.

When you take imperfect actions, you won't get the perfect result, but it's still good. It's still a result. It will get better – but not in a day or two. Your beautiful behind did not get so big in one day. Based on what theory do you think you should be the way you want a month after your wake-up call? There are middle results that only show you that you're on the right track. You're moving, advancing. Love and celebrate any results you get!

The middle results are not always what you expect. They may discourage you and even stop you from continuing. Only disregard for these results will help you be perseverant and keep going. Remember: you just have to tweak what you're doing to make it work for you.

I wonder what would've happened if I paid attention to my imperfect results? Or rather, what wouldn't have happened if I paid enough attention to how imperfect my glutes were and how awful my sagging skin looked. You know the dog breed Shar-Pei? Lots of skin, lots of resemblance. When you rapidly lose weight, your skin doesn't react as fast, especially if you're over 40. When you have clarity on that and know it's okay and it'll get better, you're at ease.

I didn't know. I was shocked. Since I never told anybody the big reasons why I was losing weight, I didn't feel like discussing it with anybody. I did share my pain with a trainer who I thought was supportive, as she was one of the few who knew of my plans. She was over 50 and told me about her deepest desire to compete and how she never did. I've noticed that, in general, when women don't realize their talents and needs, they become envious and mean. They're angry at themselves, of course, but they take it out on others.

As I was figuring out what to do about my skin and wondering whether it would go back to normal, I sent her a photo. She posted it on Instagram, calling me a stupid, aging bikini girl who had gone crazy and done this to herself. She had over a million followers, so there were tons of nice comments on my physical condition and my mental health. Do you have any idea how it feels when hundreds of unknown, mean people are criticizing your ass and making nasty comments? You don't, I hope. It's painful. For quite some time, I was thinking of how to react. I was going to explode. I wanted to call her, meet her, beat her up. I wanted revenge. You know what helped me to come to my senses and do nothing? The role we talked about. I imagined what Grace Kelly, Princess Diana, or my celebrity friend, Zhanna would do. Would they get back at that woman? Would they try to prove that she's an asshole? Would that be a Wow type of behavior? No, it wouldn't. Let it go. Life will get revenge for you. And it did – the poor woman is out of her mind now, looking terrible, angry and unfulfilled.

These are the mid-way results that are not as satisfying as we would like them to be. At this point, most people quit. They quit too soon. They give up because their expectation doesn't match the results.

Before coming to Canada in 1991, I had never been outside of Russia. I had seen movies and heard how wild the west was. I wasn't really expecting to see cowboys on the streets of Toronto, but I was definitely waiting to see the nightlife – everything open 24/7, the energy, the people, the life. I think I was expecting Las Vegas: gambling, alcohol, glamour, money, and beautiful people. We landed in Montreal on a Friday night and had to take a bus that smart Russian entrepreneurs provided since there was no direct flight from Moscow to Toronto. Strangely enough, there are still no direct flights between Russia and Canada today. I'm not sure if it's politics or economics, but I do know that it's very inconvenient.

As I was riding on the bus to Toronto that Friday night, I got very suspicious that we took the wrong route. Where's the party? Where's Vegas? Looking out the window, I saw lots of men dressed in black suits and hats, with spaghetti fringes hanging out of their jackets. In Russia, we didn't have orthodox Jewish men hanging out on the streets like that. My point is, the reality didn't match my expectations.

I think a lot of our suffering comes from the expectations we have. From the men we try to love, to the children we want to raise and the world we want to be the perfect place – our brains expect the best scenario possible. We envision it and get used to the imaginary result. We come to like it. And it's great, because visualization is at work. But then we don't perform enough actions – or even worse – worry about not getting this result. Have you ever thought that worrying is actually negative goal-setting? When we worry, we also visualize the picture in our head. Do you remember how I mentioned that the Law of Attraction is always working? It works quite well in this case too.

Ba boom! Something wrong is happening. Not wrong as in bad, but just not the way we expected it to be. Like, "Oh, honey. Really? You got me a vacuum cleaner for my birthday? How nice… but I really wanted that diamond ring we saw in the window last year. I knew it. I was worried you would fail again this time, like always."

"But darling, how was I supposed to know you wanted that ring?"

"Well, I thought you knew. You stopped and asked me if I liked that heart-shaped stone." Little did he know, he was already convicted as soon as he asked that question. He was now deemed to have performed everything possible and still didn't buy her that heart-shaped stone. He was guilty as sin just because there is a gap between what she was expecting and what she got. How many relationships have ended because of this imaginary gap? How many lives have been lived unhappily because of this hole between expectations and reality?

It's the same with our other thoughts. We expect more than we can possibly achieve. I know I said to dream the impossible, but don't set impossible expectations. We live in the real world. Let's have some common sense, too. For ages, you've been leading a not-so-healthy lifestyle. All of a sudden, you want to make a Wow coming out. Good! It's about time. Five days go by, then 10, then 21 days. You wanted to look Wow at your reunion in a month. You expected to be in great shape. You've been expecting so much. Expectations, expectations. What if you don't expect anything and just do your best? What will happen if you put aside this imagination of yours and just perform 100 percent? I bet you'll be happy with any improvements you get, any inch or kilo you lose. You'll be as surprised as a child when he sees a Christmas tree. You'll appreciate anything and everything that happens to you.

As women, what we often do is decide for everybody. For our children, we know better what they should wear and what to eat. Mama knows. Mama won't steer you wrong. But what if mama is wrong? What if she doesn't know? What if she's basing her decision on her own paradigm? Of course, most of us don't think of that. We're not aware that it's even possible. "Mama, am I hungry or thirsty now?" That's how I find a lot of men behave these days. They're dependent on their mothers' opinions and paradigms. They are infantile; they are their mothers' sons forever. They can't let go of that milk-providing breast for years, and then they find a wife to feed them that same milk. The wife was expecting to be taken care of, like her daddy took care of her (usually, as in my case). I expect a man to take care of me, as I would take care of him. I expect gifts, surprises, trips and fun. Otherwise, what's he making money for? I don't like the concept of being a very independent woman. What's so wrong with being dependent? In reality, we're all dependent on somebody: our parents, friends, colleagues, bosses. We depend on oil prices, the stock exchange, the weather. I find this concept of being modern and independent very much overrated.

A lot of women claim to be independent, and they are. They make their money, or have gained it from inheritances or ex-husbands. And then what? Most of them are bragging about the great happiness of being so independent, when in reality, they're very lonely. For some reason, they're usually bossy and tough. They lack feminine qualities. They struggle in relationships because they act somewhere between a boss, telling the man what to do, and a mother, knowing better if he's hungry or thirsty. It's okay to have some role-playing to spice things up, but in everyday life, men don't want to have sex with their mothers or bosses. (Of course, there are exceptions to any rule).

WOW WOMAN ACTION STEP 7

By now, you have your Wow clarity and contract. You know what you want. You are ready to take action – imperfect actions. You're not supposed to know for sure what is going to work, but when you take the first tiny step and succeed, you feel like a winner. This will motivate you to go further, and you will keep going, improving little by little. Some steps won't work for you, and that's great! That means you can cross that step out of your plan. To know what's not working for you is as important as knowing what is. It may even be more important, because this is how you choose your path.

Think of one little step you are going to take today.

It may be finding a gym around you, or searching for a health food store. Or maybe you'll shop for a new outfit or buy lipstick that matches your new role. If you are Marilyn Monroe, you would obviously need red lipstick, because your nude MAC won't do the job. The second step would be the dress – but today, just take that first step. Do it and celebrate. Feel like a winner. What is your first step?

_____

_____

_____

_____

_____

_____

Was that first step easy to do? Why?

_____

_____

_____

_____

_____

I'm sure it was.

This is the big secret they have been hiding from you: steps should be easy and simple. They should be small and bite-sized. It's the consistency that's harder. But for now, just feel that you did it! You are so Wow!

CHAPTER 8

How to Stop Using Fear as a Beach Cover-up

It looks like we've gathered all the main ingredients to get us where we want to be. We have a burning desire, our Wow factor, and we even got our butts off the couch and are moving towards the goal. And then our mind and body freeze. We get scared.

There are a few types of fears, with fear of death being the number one. For my audience and for myself, there's a fear of aging that's just a variety of the fear of death. Almost any woman is thinking, "Is it almost finito? How come? I haven't even started living! Stop the train! I need to get off!" But time is ruthlessly indifferent to your whining.

Any fear stops us from living the Wow life we want. It makes us small and invisible. Feelings of anxiety are also fear, just in a different format. So many of us are anxious and overwhelmed, and therefore stressed and unhappy. When we're stressed, we make decisions that don't serve us well. We lose control over our decisions and actions, meaning we lose control over our lives. We're giving away our power. In reality, fear is just a protective mechanism that has been helping us survive for so long. The older, reptile part of our brain that's in charge of our survival doesn't really care if we are happy and fulfilled. I doubt that part even knows these words. Whether I'm fulfilled or not is of no interest to that little reptile. It's only interested in keeping me alive. Because of this, we often don't take bold actions. To the brain, it means a state of alert. What does she want this time? I imagine the brain is rolling its eyes. *Try new things? Go new places? Start exercising? Oh no. Why can't she just relax? She's alive. What else does she want!?* Annoyed by your sudden activity, the brain creates all sorts of different reasons for you not to take that challenge. It's coming up with so many persuasive ideas (excuses, in reality) to stop you from challenging your present state that you give up and give in. Didn't I tell you that you are not your thoughts? Well, you aren't. And I'm not, either. I keep reminding myself of this, and I'm reminding you. Don't listen to that snake or that lizard in your head. They're only good for bags and shoes.

The condition of anxiety is nothing more than our imagination. As women, we are very creative. We create emotions, thoughts and the outcomes of the above. We create our reality. We do! Whatever happens to us, we created. And it's most often not a fairytale. It's mostly drama with some comedy elements here and there. Again, drama is always safe. It doesn't require the adventurous elements of risk and achievement.

Drama is about feeling sorry for yourself or for other people in the story. It's easy to feel bad for somebody, and to pat them on the shoulder and say, "Oh, I'm so sorry for you. It's okay that you failed. I'm sure you'll be fine," and continue doing what you were doing without really giving a flying fuck. Actually, feeling sorry is a mechanism to feel better for yourself, justifying our own unaccomplished goals and unfulfillment. By seeing somebody else fail, we somewhat give ourselves permission to fail. On the contrary, if somebody beats her laziness and fears and accomplishes her goal, that makes us almost need to conform, too. *Oh, no, why did she lose weight? Why is she looking this good? Why is she so happy? It was so safe seeing her being mediocre. Now she's Wow and that means I have to get my ass off the couch too, and I don't want to. Not that I don't want the result – I just don't want to do the work.* That reptile brain does not want change. It wants safety, remember?

Oftentimes, somebody else's accomplishments become the reason to start making changes. They become a negative/positive motivation. We get mad at her, we get angry, and then we get even. And it's great! To me, whatever works, works. It doesn't really matter what the motivating factor for the change was. What doesn't work is wanting that change so badly that we become at war with ourselves. We declare a state of war, and become warriors. I often hear women say, "I'm going to fight my fat ass and win this battle," or "I'll kill my laziness and conquer my fears." Do you notice the words you're using? They're not too peaceful, are they? They're not Wow. They are far from being sexy or joyful. Words define our actions, add meaning to what we do, and rule our reality. The vocabulary we use in our speech tells so much about our education and social standing. We should be very careful about what words we use in everyday language, as they influence and define who we are without us being aware of this impact. I talked about this a lot with my amazing writing coach, Peggy McColl. We both agreed on the importance of choosing words and phrases to manifest abundance and fulfillment. Working with people and their words, Peggy is convinced that you can figure out the mood, emotional state, struggles or joy the speaker or writer is experiencing at the moment. Therefore, you can choose your moods and state by using the most suitable language.

Think about this for a second. When you operate with phrases that show you're at war, fighting for the goal means you're fighting against somebody. Usually there are at least two sides in every war. Agreed? Most likely, that woman who negatively motivated you either doesn't know about your conquering plans, or doesn't care. She's already way ahead of you and you're not in her league. So, in reality, on the other side of the battle there is your other real enemy – and that enemy is you. (Or me. Or anybody who is fighting for the goal). Logically, if there's a war, one side is going to lose. What are the chances it's going to be you who will lose that battle? If your war is between you and you, aren't the odds of you losing 100%?

It's only when we leave the battlefield and start our improvements – not to win the fight or destroy the enemy, but by accepting the fact that we're not at war – that we can be at peace. We're whole and enough. We can release the stress and begin making life better. However, there's always room for more greatness and happiness.

I'm very proud of being told that I became an inspiration for others. Women of my age say they see some inner freedom in me and now have hope that it's not too late to start working for that body of their dreams, or quit the job they hate, or leave the husband that's not very satisfactory. It feels like they were waiting for some type of permission to make that start.

So, one day you make that decision to stop being a victim of circumstance. You finally realize that your life is 100% your responsibility and remember that you were born Wow. You are ready to reclaim your long-forgotten Wowness. I admire and applaud you for that. You don't even know yet what making a decision can do for you. By far, this is the most valuable step you can take.

I know – it looks like you haven't done much yet. You haven't made it to the gym. You haven't even gotten off the comfortable couch. You may be making this decision while having your third ice cream of the day, but it doesn't matter. All that matters is your decision.

Those who choose not to act out of fear create excuses. What do we use to cover up our fear? The most used and abused reasons are: I have no time, I have no money, I'm too young, old, fat, skinny, lazy etc.

I know them quite well, because I was an advanced user of them all.

I procrastinated a lot. Fortunately, I got to learn one great life lesson from a friend, one of the most successful athletes with millions of dollars in contracts. This was about 20 years ago. I was young and beautiful. Now I'm just beautiful, but I still remember him asking me why I didn't do any modeling.

I told him that all models are skinny. He suggested I lose some weight. I was offended and said the stupidest thing. I told him, "If someone approaches and offers me a modeling contract, I'll lose weight." I think I'd been watching too many movies. He, an NHL player making great money, looked at me with disdain and said, "Well, that's like me saying, 'Let me sign a contract with the team, and then I'll learn how to play hockey.'"

Oh my God! I was ready to hide under the table. That incident changed my life. I started actually doing things without waiting for Richard Gere on Rodeo Drive to save me.

I meet a lot of women who are still waiting and hoping to find that man who'll come and change everything. Everybody visualizes their man in good shape, easy going, fun and generous. Nobody wants a lazy, bad-mannered, boring, always stressed man. Basically, we all want a Wow man.

Visualization, as we know by now, is a great tool to get to your goals. But for some reason, we forget that there's a tiny little step of the process that can't be skipped. Disbelievers in the Law of Attraction sometimes make fun of visualization, saying you sit there by the sea, imagine, visualize – and life goes by. Somehow, everybody is forgetting that actions are the most important step in getting what we want. We don't get results from visualization alone; it just gives a sense of direction. In waiting for the Wow man, there's not much action involved on the part of these visualizing women. They want actions from men. They want them to become as close to their imagined Mr. Perfect as possible. They think it's him who has to take perfect action, it's him who has to remember that he was born Wow.

And how about you, darling? Are you Ms. Perfect? I'm not trying to offend you. I'm trying to wake you up from your beauty sleep, so you face reality. I know it's stern, but it's extremely effective. Are you in your sexy shape? How appealing do you look? How well are you taking care of yourself? Do you put crap in your mouth like there's no tomorrow? Are you stressed and overwhelmed? Are you already a Wow woman yourself? Well, you're not exactly Naomi Campbell. You probably don't have those legs. Nor are you as stylish as Ms. Beckham. You're not even close to being as successful as Oprah. (Not that you have to be like somebody, or compare). Realistically, though, are you the best version of yourself? Are you in the position to be asking that from the man you're waiting for? Honestly, why would he want to be with you in the first place!? Here's an even better question: would you want to be with yourself?

I know you may object with anger that you are a caring, loving, and honest person. Oh! And a good cook! Blah, blah, blah. Darling, let's get something straight first! He doesn't need a caring mother. (Okay, they all need one – but not at the point of first contact with you). Also, know that he can tell by his first look at you whether you're loving (if you love yourself, that is). How you love and treat yourself tells him all he needs to know. And if he can tell – and believe me, he'll know – that you don't love yourself that much (according to the way you look, you stopped loving yourself a while ago), he'll know that you can't love him if you can't even love yourself. Nobody can. As for your cooking skills, there's a cooking channel and thousands of restaurants on every corner.

The sooner you accept the truth, the faster you'll start your path to Wowness.

"Where there's a will, there's a way," they say. Now I know that if I don't have something, I simply don't want it badly enough. So often, our thought process is: *I know I should start improving my body. I need to exercise, stop eating junk, and lose weight. But my friend Laura (Natasha, Sara…fill in the blank) is even worse. She eats garbage and she's very overweight, but she's happy and men find her attractive. I'm much better looking, so I'm okay. After all, I'm 40 years old (45, 55, etc.). I'm supposed to look older and fatter!*

Let me make a note on fat here. If we call someone fat, it's often taken as offensive, but it simply means that somebody (quite often it's me) has a lot of fat on their body. You may call yourself "big boned," "husky," "plus-size," or whatever, but if you do a body composition analysis test, or if we put you on an X-ray machine, the truth about your big bones will come out. And so will the truth about the big-boned belly that's hanging over the jeans. If my body fat percentage is increasing, I'm getting fat, and it needs to be decreased with nutrition and exercise.

Besides age, there's another convenient excuse: kids. The common paradigm I hear is, "I gave birth. I'm a mother! I'm supposed to have a belly. I've given birth three, four, five times!" Okay, you gave birth – but so did 70 percent (I assume) of all women. Are they all out of shape? No. You gave birth to a child; you have not eaten them, hopefully. Why should you look like you did?

Unfortunately, I have only one child, so I'm not an expert. But when I did one of my fitness competitions, I met a woman who had six kids. She was going through a terrible divorce and custody battle. At that time, she didn't have custody. Her kids were living with their father until the final decision. These fitness bikini competitions were her way of dealing with everything life was throwing at her. She had six kids, was 48, and looked amazing.

There are lots of examples of famous, beautiful women who gave birth and look fabulous. We spy on them on TV, in magazines or on Instagram. They shine and motivate. Those witches! They annoy and irritate us. Secretly, we admire and try to be like them, but we're full of excuses. As we run out of superficial reasons, we use this one: "She has money," we say. "She can afford to invest in herself."

Money, money, money – my favorite subject. (Right after men).

If we think about it, it's unbelievable how much money and how many resources we invest in our egos, buying cars, clothes, jewelry, etc. We feed our egos to get some temporary satisfaction, some feeling of belonging and accomplishment. Vanity is such a costly personality trait to feed! A few months ago, I was moving to a new place and had to go through my storage unit, where I kept stuff – *lots* of stuff, that is. Bags, shoes, suits. Chanel, Dior, Valentino. For so long, I've been investing in things that temporarily satisfy some ego need. I'm not against beautiful things. I love expensive clothes. I love jewelry. After all, my father was a jeweler. I grew up among diamonds and emeralds. But what I realize now is that I couldn't really afford all those material things from a financial, logical standpoint. Why did I buy myself a $3,000 dress when I had only $10,000 in my bank account? Who did I want to impress? What did I have to prove? Now, most of the time, I think like an investor – like a man.

Let's imagine that you can have anything you want: the Bugatti of your dreams, the biggest pink diamond on your finger, or whatever else your heart may desire. You're driving down the road and enjoying yourself, but the rules of your imaginary game state that there are no people to see it. Nobody can look at you and say, "Wow, she's nailed it! She knows how to live. She knows something I don't." There's nobody to envy you, nobody to hate you. How long will you enjoy these wonderful accomplishments? Your vain ego won't be happy for long, will it? What will make you – the real you – happy?

I know what makes me happy. I like getting up early in

the morning and doing the things I choose to do. Mornings have a special power in them. They are virgin, naive, fresh and vibrant. They are free and powerful. And because I am the only one awake this early, they're totally mine. I love using these mornings to do the work I love, studying, listening to podcasts, reading smart and motivating books, writing this (or another book, perhaps), doing fast cardio, going for a long, very romantic walk with myself. I love that morning solitude. Also, doing this regimen puts me in the role of a winner for the whole day. I try accomplishing as many important tasks as I can. Then I congratulate myself on the wins. I celebrate it with a few cups of coffee, preferably with MCT oil, and go through the day like a winner. Try it – it works! Of course, for some of you, evenings may have this power. It doesn't matter. Whatever works for you is the best plan.

Another very important thing that makes me happy is that I can't really call my work a "job." I just don't like the word "job." I don't like when people say, "I lost a job." To me, it's like losing an important part of yourself. I've never lost a job, so I don't know. It must be hard when your life, and, most importantly, the life of your family, depends on some boss who woke up on the wrong foot. "There goes my family vacation, my child's dance lessons, and my parent's cottage renovations down the drain." In reality, though, that dependency on his wrong foot was a decision you might have made once. You may have chosen some fake stability over the risk of becoming your own boss, and now you pay. We always pay for our decisions, or we get rewarded.

A woman wrote me about how devastated she was with her body and looks. She told me that on a scale from

1 to 10, her pain was more like 12, and she needed my help. Since I run an online group program, the investment in her well-being through me and my coaching was very insignificant. She told me she had to ask her husband for the money. At first, I said okay. Then I changed my mind and wrote her back, "Please don't. I won't take you as my client. You don't have a body issue; you have a relationship and money problem. To me, if you have to ask permission to be happy (because this is your big Wow factor) you first have to work on your self-confidence and self-sufficiency." I now have a self-confidence course, but at that time, she was trying to solve her weight issue through my nutrition program. I knew her husband would be telling her whether or not she was allowed to follow my recommendations. No, thank you. I have the privilege to choose clients who find ways to work with me if it's their priority.

I had another potential client who told me she was very upset that she did not have enough money to hire a coach and ease her pain of being heavy, and therefore, was uncomfortable and unhappy with herself. Then I saw her Instagram page, and she was bragging about a new pair of Louboutin boots she just bought. Nice. Don't get me wrong. You're talking to a shoe addict. This addiction is costly, but satisfying. I am far from perfect and have my flaws. Of course, I don't blame or judge her – but what's happening here is not lack of money, but a matter of priorities. I just love the book by Mark Manson, *The Subtle Art of Not Giving a Fuck*. I totally agree that we don't have to give a fuck about things that are not important to us. Yes, we're allowed to not care. We have our own permission. So why wouldn't you just admit that, at this time, handling your problem isn't important to you? You don't want to improve your body, your health or your quality of life. Those

$2,000 shoes are more important for your Wow right now. You just want the shoes, and that's totally fine, girl.

You don't exercise because you work too many hours and don't have time, right? I'm running out of excuses, but time is another big one on the list. Is time really an issue? Or is the issue that exercising is not your priority? You don't care strongly enough about the way you look and feel to do something about it. For a busy, professional woman, it's normal not to have time for some absolutely unimportant task.

We will always be lacking money, support, knowledge etc. When are you going to stop creating excuses? You're a grown-ass woman! Do you know that you're free not to exercise simply because you don't want to? But, if the gap between what you really want and what you claim you want is making you unhappy, then act. If it's not, just enjoy your shoes, cake and ice cream. Don't stress about anything. Relax. By the way, when you're relaxed, you lose weight easier.

Another role that most of us women immerse ourselves in is the position of an obliger. I admire the work of Gretchen Rubin on this. She has a law background like me, and she also became a writer. She's interested in habits, making choices, behavior, accountability and thought processes. She's helping people become happy, and that's why I can relate. We listen and trust people like us. We can be coached by people who went through the same challenges and won. Gretchen has written about our roles. She calls them tendencies. Her book, *The Four Tendencies*, is about personality profiles that reveal how to make our lives better. You can take an online test Gretchen offers. If you feel like you have been investing your life in others – kids, families and men – and now you're feeling tired, empty, unsatisfied and drained, I bet you are an obliger.

Obligers, as Gretchen points out, readily meet expectations imposed on them by others, but struggle to meet the expectations they want to impose on themselves. They excel at meeting other people's demands and deadlines. They put other people's needs – family, clients, friends – ahead of their own. They easily make time for other people, but not for themselves. Sound familiar? Do you have a project or goal you struggle to work on? Do you miss your massage or yoga class? I'm sure you do. Do you have a paradigm that promises made to yourself can be broken? Everything and everybody else is always more important.

If you are this type of woman, what do you do? Do you change your nature? Or do you accept that that's the way it is, and give up? Nope. You find ways to cope with that. Once you know yourself, you need a good strategy. One of the main things to be done for an obliger is to pick the right kind of accountability. It should be to an actual person that you respect and value. You can partner with a classmate, trainer, coach, healthcare worker, teacher, family member, etc. Group Coaching programs such as weight loss or other goal achievement programs work better for obligers. I know – I run group transformational programs. I love to see how women transform, and how they start making their own needs and happiness a priority! These women are much more responsible and perform way better in a group because they have promised to perform in front of the group. Also, they get support from other women with the same goals and struggles. Others prefer individual coaching, as long as there's someone to look over their shoulder and give them the magic kick in the butt. And I'm good at that.

I quite often feel I'm more of an upholder. Upholders have a much easier time meeting both inner and outer expectations. I don't think I was born with that; I feel like it's an acquired skill. But there are times when I fall back into my obliging tendency. I need that outside support and that swift kick to meet the deadline.

I think part of these different types of behaviors has to do with self-love. Plain old self-love, which is the root cause of a lot of our problems, and, simultaneously, the reason behind success and happiness. Those two, by the way, are not synonyms. Not all successful people are happy and vice versa. Of course, it depends how you define success. Usually, we mean accomplished financial or career goals. To me, happiness is my success, and in order to be happy, I have to practice self-care. My logic is that if you love and respect yourself enough, you won't miss your training session, your cardio, or your massage. You'll give attention and energy to things that are import-ant to you. If you aren't your first priority, how can you take care of somebody else? I know it's tough. A lot of us were brought up with the idea that it is egotistical and not very nice for a good girl to be selfish, that we have to please others and care for them more than we care for ourselves. Otherwise, we're not "good" people.

I had a client with a severe weight issue that was causing her lots of health complications. We were working on finding her Why, but as we kept digging in to find that Wow factor, I felt like we weren't getting anywhere. As a very intelligent and financially successful woman, she fully understood that all her unhealthy habits had caused her health condition to worsen. It constricted her lifestyle. She couldn't spend active time with her little daughter, and that really bothered her, because her main value was to be a great mother. She clearly understood that the worst thing that could happen to her was death. I tried pushing on that pain point. "What will happen if you die? Who will raise your daughter?" I asked. "Her father," she said, without hesitation. "He's a great father."

I was stunned, but I kept pushing. "Her father will eventually re-marry a beautiful, young woman who will become a new mother to your daughter!" I was expecting a grand finale with her breakdown and, therefore, a breakthrough. I was shocked when that didn't happen.

"That's okay. They all deserve to be happy," she told me. And that was her choice. I disagreed with that choice, but that is just me. I rest my case.

WOW WOMAN ACTION STEP 8

Can you describe your biggest fear?

_____

_____

_____

_____

_____

_____

_____

What are you actually afraid of?

_____

_____

_____

_____

_____

What's the worst thing that will happen to you when you do that scary but important thing?

_____

_____

_____

_____

_____

_____

What will happen if you don't do it? Which one of those two outcomes motivates you more?

_____

_____

_____

_____

_____

_____

Choose an important task. Make a decision to focus on it. Put it on your calendar. What is it?

_____

_____

_____

_____

_____

_____

It doesn't matter if it's a training session or a manicure. It's something of importance to you, and you don't need any justification for it, because you are important to yourself, right?

Deciding to make yourself a priority, making those appointments in your calendar and marking them a top priority slowly but surely builds that very needed self-love.

Imagine that scheduled appointment is with someone really important – some authority. It could be anybody. Let's pretend it's Mr. Putin. It doesn't matter how you personally view him; you wouldn't miss an appointment with him, right? I wouldn't. I tried making that appointment, but he never replied. It's probably because he doesn't know that I was born Wow.

CHAPTER 9

How to Wake Up With a Loved One — Your Body!

B ased on knowledge and experience, I'm a true believer that until a woman is comfortable in her own skin and body, she can't be truly fulfilled or satisfied in other areas of her life. By nature, women have an innate skill to take care of the house. While her man is hunting in the woods (or office), she prepares food for herself and her family. She takes care of the household and makes sure there's comfort and tidiness. Of course, the social norms have shifted enormously, but the natural call is still there, regardless of whether she does it herself or with the help of a skilled housekeeper. This idea of a house as a safe and cozy place has to exist for her to function at her best. But before this outer world, there's her own sacred home – the body itself. This is a shelter she can always escape to when reality becomes harsh and stressful. Logically, this sacred place should be taken care of in the best possible way. She should clean it, like she does her little *Desperate Housewives* house. She has decorated her house with flowers, pictures, inspirational quotes in white frames, soft pillows, and inviting fireplaces. Isn't it strange that we're willing and happy to improve the outside space around us, but when it comes to our own bodies, we don't do these home improvements as enthusiastically (or don't do them at all?) A lot of us have one thing in common: we want to change. We agree that we need to change. And, as smart and educated women, we have gathered an enormous amount of information so that we can begin that change. We have a massive load of knowledge in our heads, but because we're so overwhelmed with information, we get paralyzed and don't know where to start.

When you're over forty and have been postponing your own needs, starting is the hardest part. By now, we've created a love/hate relationship with our safe and sacred place. This relationship is often so intense and destructive that we suffer. We intentionally or unintentionally (for me, it's subconsciously intentional for some hidden reason) destroy our temple instead of loving and caring for it. How we look and feel is completely up to every one of us. It's a choice we make, and these choices are different. It pains me to see how women give away their power to that ice cream or that bag of chips. When we can't say no to that greasy, cheesy burger, the burger is ruling our lives. We aren't ruling the burger. Do I want my life to be run by this melting, fattening creature that some business entity created and sold me so they could make a profit? No, I don't.

But, honestly, sometimes I do. Sometimes I let my life be run by a burger. And, believe it or not, it's okay to have a burger once in a while, just as it's totally fine to have ice cream, chips and fries. If I totally limit myself from burger love, I get a feeling of self-hatred and guilt if I can't resist the melting fat. If I totally refuse one food or another, they have even more power over me, because they've managed to cut me off from my own reality.

That's probably the reason I don't follow any particular way of eating. I don't like putting labels on myself or others. I feel like it limits our main freedom to choose our reality. Once I pronounce myself vegan, I have to live by it every minute of my life, because I value and respect my decision. To me, it's unlikely that we can be that strict with ourselves. And the main question is, what for? It's okay to have plant-based food. It's okay to enjoy raw food. But if I have a great cooked steak one day, is this supposed to make me feel like a loser – like I've failed my commitment and betrayed my label? Why create those restrictions if we can create everyday choices that are best for the body and the soul? Like anything else, it takes time to master making the best choice every time you choose a meal, but you get rewarded by feeling comfortable in your own body – and that feels incredible.

The notion of us ruling and creating our world is more appealing to me than the idea of having total control over something. The more we control something, the more tension we bring to the situation. If we control how much to eat and what to drink, we become like soldiers. Control is harsh, demanding, and masculine. My father (God rest his soul), was a very controlling man. He wanted to control me, my brother and the whole family. Most importantly, he always wanted to control his body. He exercised for as long as I can remember – boxing, tennis, running. Having done acrobatics in his youth, he could do amazing things with his body even in his fifties. He told me that body control was one of the most important values in his life. And then he died at 54. He was looking young and feeling healthy, but he died, ironically, having lost the control of his body.

He had a horrifying disease called ALS – Amyotrophic Lateral Sclerosis (or Lou Gehrig's disease). It's a motor neuron disease that gradually paralyzes people because their brain is no longer in communication with their body. A person with this condition loses the ability to walk, talk, eat, swallow, and finally, breathe. Basically, the person is losing control of their own body. My dad was so afraid of this; his worst nightmare came true.

There's no treatment for ALS. Even cancer is somewhat treatable if caught in early stages. Here, you are given a diagnosis and you wait. The wait is usually two years. And that's it – there's nothing you can do. The worst part is that the person's brain is still perfectly fine. It's working at its full ability and trying to find anything that can help, Googling day and night to find help that doesn't exist. And then you realize you can't control it anymore.

I think when you put your focus on your fear, you give that fear energy. You nurture it, and then fear dictates the reality you create. I feel this is what happened to my dad.

The notion of creating our world derives from a different position – a position of love. It then becomes a creative process, an art, a mastery, and you become a Master. Love is inspirational, light and feminine. It's pleasant, joyful. When we focus on love, we're not scared. We influence, motivate and inspire. And that's what Masters do.

When we choose a position for our action, we also choose the method – the means of transforming the world around us. Let's admit it: we all want to feel important. We want to bring something into this world, leave a mark, and do something significant. We basically want to save the world. Like Baywatch lifeguards with their hair flying in the wind, we tend to imagine how we'll look in that red bikini, doing something really important for the world. But the world is on hold because we don't fit into that bikini. We're not ready to save anybody.

To tell you the truth, I've always loved my face – even my snub nose – in spite of my father making fun of it and saying he's ready to pay for a nose job. But I've never been too comfortable in my own skin with some parts of my body. I could never fully accept and love it the way it was. I didn't like my wide hips, my square ass. I was stupid enough not to like my size D cups. They were the biggest of all the girls in my class. I had difficulties performing some running and jumping exercises in the gym. The teacher was a lonely, retired athlete who was totally unrealized in her sports ambitions. She had no kids or family and no sports trophies to speak of. She took that out on us, the students. I was forced to wear a tight white shirt that showed everything. My father also thought it revealed too much. One day, he came home and handed me something. "Take it," he said. He turned around, turned red, and looked away. That's how I got my first bra.

Women often write to applaud and appreciate me for how open and honest I am about my flaws. I'm not ashamed to post before and after pics. I often make fun of those imperfections because I've learned to accept them. Now I'm proud to show the end results after all the work I've done. One of the first steps to making something better is to accept the naked truth about your naked body. Unfortunately, we cover it up with fancy clothes and expensive surgeries.

Be aware that if you want me to help you transform your body, I'll ask you to accomplish one rather harsh task: take a picture of yourself almost naked, just in your underwear – front and back. Try it. It's hard. For some– really hard. You don't have to show it to me. It's your own pain. Looking at that cellulite and sagging skin is painful. That's where a lot of women (and men, believe it or not) give up. They can't accept the truth. I have homework to be done every week in my coaching program, and I've had people disappear on me after they received this assignment, even having paid me big bucks for coaching! Of course, they'd been hiding the reality from themselves for so long, covering up with designer pareos in the summer and sable furs in winter. Or diamonds. They always work as a great cover-up to hide the pain for a while. Five carats and up does wonders. But like makeup will never help with acne, no cover-up will help to really heal your temple – your body!

It's my absolute belief, based on my own experience and on what I see with my clients, that until we accept the truth and the reality of our present physical and mental condition, we won't be able to move forward to bigger goals and achievements. And there's no standard for that – we all begin at different standpoints.

I'm sure you're dying to know how my own transfor- mation started, and the answer is, the exact same way! I just took a picture of my behind. My girlfriend did it. She's a very business-oriented woman, and for some reason she said that this photo would make us money one day. Well, she was so damn right on this point! The acceptance of truth will set you free. Back then, though, I cried. I was mad. Actually, I was furious. Then I slowly learned to accept that truth.

I know a lot of women are investing their time and money in learning about nutrition and fitness. It's a trend now. It's in fashion, and we like to be trendy and fashion-able. A few years back, the trend was to be a designer. Now we want to be nutrition specialists. I'm not an exception; I like to be trendy. Only, one little component that's very often missing is the implementation. Women talk about macro and micronutrients at dinner. They discuss gluten intolerance at lunch. They even talk about ATP cycles, BMI and other bizarre abbreviations. But when it comes time to apply that knowledge, they back off. They tell me they're postponing it until the right time. What right time? There's no such thing.

May I offer you a termination to the endless search for the new "it" thing – the new pill, the new magic diet? May I tell you that you know enough already for the trans-formation itself? You do. You know it yourself. You may feel lost and overwhelmed by that knowledge, but the feeling of overwhelm won't go away if you learn "just a little more." Improve your own professional knowledge – be a better cook, lawyer, librarian. Not everybody must become a trainer and a nutrition specialist. For you, the beginner, there are only a few things needed and you don't have to get certified for that (unless you feel it's your mission to help others go through these transformations, as it is mine).

Those who have chosen the right time to be today have one thing in common: the fear of what's going to happen if they don't start taking care of themselves urgently is greater than the fear of the change itself. In their self-talk, they ask themselves absolutely eye-opening questions: How am I going to feel if I miss this opportunity today? How will I look a year from now? How will I look in five years? Old? Invisible? Sick? Lonely? If you imagine what can happen and that picture is creepy enough, you'll start your transformation. I remember how scared I was imagining that I'd feel and look worse and worse every month, or even every day. Don't want that anymore, do you?

If you've started your journey to Wowness, congratulations – but you know what happens to a lot of us? We want results. Now. Today. Yesterday is even better. For the last five years, you were eating your guts out, sitting on your ass, and trying to find the perfect routine for yourself. Of course, you now feel tired from trying to figure out the most suitable path without even making it to the gym yet. I understand. I've been there. Doesn't it feel like you've already gone through all the low-fat, low-carb, gluten-free, lectin-free, raw, and vegan diets you read about?

Haven't you (mostly in your mind), done CrossFit, HIIT, LISS, Yoga and Pilates? I have. Don't you feel tired from all those thoughts, theories and ideas running their cardio through your mind? A lot of us are. That's why a lot of us are stressed even before we start doing something in reality. We want the results of our physical workout to happen as fast as the results of our thought process. Can I remind you that the speed of those two is different?

I see you've started to eat "properly," whatever that means. I don't like words like proper, right, ideal, or perfect. I honestly don't know what that is. Please introduce me to somebody who knows. As we're all smart and educated here, let's think logically. Let's think like a man. (Okay, some men).

If there are thousands of different types of quick-fix diets, doesn't it mean that they don't work?

Otherwise, what's the point of coming up with another thousand? When the bicycle was invented the way it was, no other types came out. We may add a wheel or two, but that's an upgrade for some variety. The light bulb is another example. It's still the same, because it still gives light. It solves the problem. It works. There's no need to reinvent the wheel or the light bulb. Every diet doesn't solve the problem, or the solution is temporary. If we only want that change for one important day, like for your high school reunion, to prove you're still as hot as you were at 17, and you don't care about the rest, then that's okay.

I'm sure you've tried all sorts of diets. Can we talk, expert to expert, about weight loss diets? What was your favorite? My preference was the cabbage soup diet. The smell of that soup is still in my sensory memory. One of the seven days of that diet, I had to eat eight bananas and milk. As an expert, I'm sure you've tried it, too. Aren't you laughing now? Oddly enough, we're still searching for yet another diet! But why would we need to, if that cabbage worked so well? Or was it the milk? Did it really do your body good?

WOW WOMAN ACTION STEP 9

I am challenging you to perform the same exercise that temporarily destroyed my state of mind and then graced me with transformation. Take a picture of yourself naked. Take a look at it. Meet and greet it, maybe for the first time. Talk to it, and find what you like about it. Yes, there IS something you like. Find things that could be improved, without judgement. Look at it from the position of, "Oh, how interesting. I have a birthmark," or "I have dimples. Is that what they call cellulite, I wonder?" By the way, almost all of us real women have that. It's okay. Even those skinny supermodels have it. They've been Photoshopped enormously. You, on the other hand, are true and real.

This is how your own transformation can start. It's like Alcoholics Anonymous. I've never been to a meeting, but I watch movies.

So, darling, first you accept reality. Cry out loud, suffer, go into a depression mode for a while. It's all good. It will help you get moving!

You may hate me for this, but I don't care. It's not about me; it's about you. I want you to change.

You can send me champagne (Cristal, please) later.

Measure your level of happiness with your body. It's easy to test.

Just answer this: how happy are you with the way your body is on a scale of 1 to 10? What would you like to change or improve?

_____

_____

_____

_____

_____

_____

_____

_____

_____

_____

_____

_____

_____

_____

_____

_____

_____

_____

You know. We always do.

Be honest. It's time to change that.

You were born Wow, but then you forgot to take care of your Wowness. We all do that. You're not alone.

CHAPTER 10

The Agony of Deception and the Ecstasy of Ease

It's true that I'm a certified fitness nutrition specialist, twice certified health coach and fitness trainer. To better serve my target audience, I even became a hormone specialist so that I could help women more. But all this knowledge would mean nothing if I hadn't tested everything I learned on myself: the fat loss and muscle gain, Keto, low-carb, high-fat, gluten-free, wheat-free, and sugar-free. The cardio, weights, CrossFit, Pilates, running, swimming, dancing. I've tried them all. Through this hands-on approach, I've come to some conclusions, and one of them is that it's all much easier than we're led to believe. Let me say it again: it's much easier than we're led to believe. You have been deceived. Me too.

In reality, every creator of a new approach is selling us the one and only "proper" way to eat and exercise, in their view. I remember, when visiting Japan, that I went to see the famous Japanese rock garden in Kyoto. It was a square landscape with sand and big rocks of different shapes and sizes. To sit and watch the stones is considered a meditative practice for those trying to find a higher meaning of life, and a way to become aware of something that's invisible.

There are 15 mysterious stones, laid out so that all the stones can't be seen at the same time. People sit around this landscape trying to see what's not visible. They may be sitting there for hours, looking and looking, thinking and thinking, meditating and meditating. Some write down genius thoughts and ideas on where that 15th stone is. I'm very much in favor of meditation and other practices that help us achieve our goals and go through life joyfully, but I don't like when people overcomplicate things and make a mountain out of a small hill. I like to help people make their lives easier, not harder. I enjoy helping you get out of overwhelm.

It's the same with food and exercise. To me, everything is blown out of proportion. There are hundreds of different diets and ways of eating, and hundreds of methods for exercising. There is scientifically-proven research for every one of those theories. And there are others, equally scientific, that prove them wrong. We don't know who to trust or what to believe, especially when most of it is sponsored by big corporations that need to sell their product. For exactly the same reasons, I personally don't adopt any particular way of eating or a certain fitness routine – maybe because I've tried lots and realized they may or may not work, depending on a hundred personal factors. Maybe it's because in my health coaching school, I was fortunate to be introduced to the concept of "bio-individuality." This notion states that we're all different in gender, age, occupation, activity and exercise levels, so very distinctive approaches should be used to solve a problem.

For example, when I was preparing for my competition, I ate five to six meals per day. Complex carbohydrates were added to three or four of them. Since I was already doing health coaching, I insisted that the women I was helping lose weight have oats for breakfast, or a disaster would strike and they'd have no energy for the whole day. The breakfast issue was coming up very often. I had strong views on that, but people had well-established habits. Some didn't want to eat in the morning. Since a health coach is actually a master of habit change, I was helping those poor no breakfast people break that terrible pattern. At the time, I was doing at least one hour of cardio a day and one hour of weight training. I used "good" carbs for energy.

It was working for me pretty well, until I became a different bio-individual myself, having stopped my extensive fitness hours and strict shredding processes. After three years of competing, I said enough, because my "Why" wasn't there any longer. There were no more compelling reasons to do the strict diet for months, no inner motivation to invest enormous amounts of time in the process. As I was walking with my daughter one night in Miami, she asked me to get an ice cream. Obviously, I couldn't have any ice cream myself because it was shredding time for my competition. At that moment, I was faced with a dilemma. I asked myself, "What's more important – to go on stage and feed my ego once again, or to be a fun-loving mother to my daughter?" That very moment, I chose to be a mother and eat a chocolate ice cream. Two ice creams, in fact.

As I've revaluated my priorities and changed the competitive athlete role to a "normal," stress-free, not hungry, not constantly exhausted mother, my eating habits had to change accordingly. Another lifestyle alteration was going to happen because I made a decision to get a bunion removed from my foot, something I'd been postponing for years.

If you've had a bunion, you know the pain. It's almost like a toothache, the only difference being that you have to walk on it. And also do squats and run miles – nevermind heels. My dream was to actually walk all the way from the car to the venue and not hide my ballerina shoes in my purse. So, I got my surgery done.

I have an amazing doctor. Write me if you want this pain relief. No scars, no downtime. Just an ugly boot for six weeks and six more weeks with no heels. It's easy to suffer a little for an awaited end goal.

What's not easy, and definitely not recommended, is to make drastic changes in everything at once. From a toned and shredded athlete, in a matter of a week, you become a "regular" 44-year-old woman. And how do a lot of "regular" women feel? Fat, unattractive, maybe depressed because they're not feeling comfortable with their own bodies; they don't look and feel how they want to. What's worse is that they know they're capable of doing something about it, because when it comes to things outside of their own needs, they're very successful. But when it comes to their own inner comfort, they're ready to give up trying. They feel angry and powerless.

I know a lot of us have felt like that for years. We may even have gotten used to these feelings and they've numbed down a little. But if you've experienced the comfort of being your absolute best naked, if you've been shot by well-known photographers on Malibu Beach in your tiniest bikini, while bystanders take pictures of you, you'd know that going back to "regular" is tough.

Now I'm a more experienced fitness bikini competitor, so I know what to expect, but when the first competition was over, I just let myself go. Not for months – just for five days! I felt like I deserved this treat because I was such a good girl. I am sure you can relate. You know that "I was good, so I deserve…" state of mind, right? Only five days after I competed, I was too ashamed to get out of bed, because I was feeling fat. I was feeling like a balloon, ready to explode. I know it's hard to believe, but that's what happens to the body when you stop exercising and dieting after the contest and indulge in all the wonderful, sweet things you were refusing yourself for so long.

I allowed myself to have a food party, for only five freaking days! When shooting on a beach that I scheduled after the competition, naively thinking I would stay in that shape forever, I had to cover up my abs, as there weren't any showing. Another few days later, I took a 12-hour flight, and by the time we landed, my legs were huge. I couldn't get into my shoes – that's how swollen they were from the knees down. Ten days later, I couldn't get out of bed as I was going through a deep depression. People have expectations of the way you are supposed to look, from seeing you on stage and on social media. They want to see you in person. They want to touch you. They want to see you at your gym and (hopefully), congratulate you on your achievement. But you can't get your ass to the gym, because it's huge and fat, and you feel and look ugly.

We oftentimes lose connection with our bodies and consider them to be a separate entity. We're somewhat in denial that our body belongs to us, and that's why we let it go. *What? That fat ass? No, it's not me. I'm not responsible for it.* In reality, the body is much smarter than we think, and at the same time, believe it or not, it is a part of us. If you've been trying to deprive it of calories, it may want revenge. It's not acting against your wishes; it's fighting for your safety, trying to keep the homeostasis of your well-being.

Remember, the mind and body don't care about your ego; they just want you to be alive. This is the same reason that your miraculous ten-day diet doesn't work. Once your brain gets an alert that you're in the danger zone, it wants to prepare you for unforeseen circumstances. It begins to store all your calories to protect you.

This last time after the competition, I had more experience and, therefore, more control, but I still gained some weight and that stressed me a lot. I decided to try something new – something that would go against my five-times-a-day religion with oatmeal for energy. I tried a high-fat, low-carb way of eating and combined it with intermittent fasting. My food for the day was a lot of healthy fats: avocado, wild salmon, nuts and seeds. I also had some occasional unhealthy fats, such as bacon, but it was still fat and didn't raise my insulin level. That's the main point of the high-fat, low-carb diet. I loved this way of eating. I had coffee in the morning and no food until around 2 p.m. Then there was an eight-hour window where I ate two or three meals.

In a week, I noticed my stress level had decreased substantially. I became much calmer and didn't react to life pressures as I usually would. That alone is an unbelievable accomplishment, because stress influences our lives enormously. A lot of us don't even realize the correlation between stress and weight loss, or sleep and weight gain. How many of us are trying to get out of stressful situations with pills and some special techniques that take a lot of effort and investment?

In reality, if we could just manage the food we eat, there are so many easy life-saving answers. Too bad people don't believe this. We'd rather invest in some expensive technologies than control what we eat. Don't you find it ironic that as easy as it is to do something, it's just as easy not to do it? For example, it's so easy to drink water. There's nothing to it. It's on every corner, it's available, and it's cheaper than your Starbucks latte. Yet, almost everybody has a problem with water intake. "Oh, it's so difficult. It's so inconvenient." Yet, those same people invest thousands in moisturizing creams and mud wraps. Strange, isn't it? Just drink your water and skip the mud.

Even though it was great to be serene and relaxed, my goal was to lose weight (or rather, that fat feeling), in the absence of movement because of the bunion surgery. But I didn't. Why not? There were no insulin spikes, and my hormonal system was working perfectly well. The quality of food was great. Water intake was okay. So why didn't I lose weight? I overate. Plain and simple. Calories – the ones I started counting as a teenager. Years and countless diet theories later, the plain and simple importance of calorie intake is not outdated after all. The simple fact is, if you take in more calories than you burn, you'll gain weight. The great news is that when you consume a lot of healthy fats, your appetite decreases substantially. Therefore, you automatically eat less and don't feel hungry. In my case, though, I was overeating not because of physical hunger, but because of mental boredom. I was not used to being limited in my movement, so with my recovering leg, I made slow but frequent promenades to the refrigerator.

Lately, we've discovered a lot of interesting information on what's "bad" for you, and women are lost and stressed. They're freaking out. "So what do I eat? If everything is so bad for you, what's 'good' for you? Where do I start if I want to become healthy and happy?" Not trying to be perfect is one answer, and clean eating is another. I'm a firm believer that until you make your food as clean as possible, you may as well not bother with anything else. Clean eating is the essence of any diet.

Like the water example, clean eating is so easy to achieve; yet it's not done by most. What is clean eating, anyway? I would say it's food that is the least touched by humans, by the manufacturer, or by the profit beneficiary, because that's who's dictating what you put in your mouth. Everything that's packaged, canned or boxed with two or more ingredients is not clean. All food that's "good" for you has one or two ingredients. An apple is an apple. A piece of beef is a piece of beef. It's one ingredient. When there's a list of ingredients I can't read or pronounce, my guess is maybe I don't need that. I'll say it again: if I don't even know what that is, my body probably doesn't want to find out.

The alarming information on the damage that sugar does just won't fit in this chapter. Cutting sugar is another very important thing you can do to improve your life substantially. The most damaging thing is that we're not aware of what we're consuming. "Do you eat sugar?" I ask my clients. They look at me like I just accused them of first-degree murder. "Me? Of course not. I take care of myself," my clients say proudly.

When I mention honey, ketchup or dried peaches as other types of sugars, they're surprised. Most of us are unaware of the amount of sugar we're really eating. It's the same thing with calories. We are disillusioned when it comes to the amount of food we consume. We tend to undervalue those amounts. Consciously and unconsciously, we hide it from ourselves, but it reveals itself on our hips and bellies. And then we're surprised! Where did it come from?

"I gained weight from air!" we say. Then I ask people to write down everything they eat. Surprise, surprise: healthy fats have lots of calories!

Until you manage the quality and quantity of the food you enjoy, don't get yourself into timing, frequency and other more difficult tasks to manage. Try to make your food as clean as possible and increase your calorie consumption awareness. It doesn't have to be perfect and forever. With time, your awareness will become second nature and your taste buds won't accept the mayo that you thought you couldn't live without. Donuts won't be something you crave. It will happen one day. Be prepared, as it takes time and patience.

You probably know that nutrition is about 80% of success in getting the body and health you want. Exercise, sleep and stress make up the rest. I regret being in denial of this for too long, thinking I could get in shape by just doing some cardio work. Why didn't I just accept this earlier?

When it comes to exercising, especially for those of us who haven't started until now, or are not happy with the results, we're trying to find the perfect regiment. But perfection doesn't exist. What exists is what you do on a regular basis for an extended period. The type, intensity and quantity of your exercise depends entirely on your starting point, your goals and your commitment. Please don't compare yourself to anybody else, that kills everything. Choose any type of activity you enjoy doing – unless you're very serious about getting more than just a body to be comfortable in, or unless your goals are to be more of an athlete. In that case, you'll have to do something you might not enjoy very much so that you can get where most other people won't. But let's assume you aren't going to compete. Just enjoy your favorite activity and gradually increase time and frequency. For example, I love salsa and belly dancing, and I also absolutely fell in love with weights. Actually, I fell in love with the results first, and loving the process came later. I may just be lucky that way. On the other hand, I absolutely don't like CrossFit or meditative yoga. But I do like Bikram yoga, because you simultaneously get your heart pumped and stretch. We're all different. It's okay to try diverse activities. It's okay to love some and detest others. Try High-intensity interval training. It's one of the best ways of training I have found for myself and my new goals. It saves me time and mental energy, and totally suits my not-so-athletic lifestyle.

There are many things you can do to get that look and feel you always wanted. One thing you can't do is do nothing and expect different results. It sounds like such a simple idea, but for some reason we just don't get it. How can we expect different results from doing the same things? That just won't happen. Act differently, and the results will be visible and very satisfying in the mirror.

WOW WOMAN ACTION STEP 10

Do you really realize what you eat? Are you aware of the effect some foods have on your body?

How do you react to dairy? For example, I always ate dairy, without being aware that it blocks my sinuses with mucus and my stomach gets bloated. I didn't know milk could talk. I hear it, and so do others close to me. The growling is pretty loud and not sexy at all. I considered milk to be healthy, but it betrayed me.

_____

_____

_____

_____

_____

How do you react to wheat? Personally, I just love croissants, but I've noticed that I get a sore throat after. I used to think I was catching a cold. And again, I get bloated.

How about water intake? How much do you drink? Measure it. It will most likely be less than you think.

_____

_____

_____

_____

_____

How many calories do you consume in general? Upload one of the apps for calorie counting. Learn how to use it. Put in everything you eat for a few weeks. Get an understanding of what four ounces of chicken is, what 100 grams of cooked oats is. Before figuring out how much you should be enjoying, find out what you are eating now. Become aware of your starting point. Be surprised by how much you actually consume – and then decrease it for weight loss.

_____

_____

_____

_____

_____

_____

_____

_____

_____

_____

_____

_____

Awareness is a huge part of your success. Don't worry, you don't have to measure this your whole life. Your beautiful eyes will soon become your food scale.

When you finally have that true picture of what you put in your mouth, make some adjustments and enjoy the Wow health and Wow body you were born with.

CHAPTER 11

Image: Portray What You Want to Convey

When I first came to Canada, I was 17. I was young and daring, and I was wearing heels: black patent four-inch heels. I also had a short dress and a white jacket on. Can you imagine long travel hours looking this sharp? Neither can I now. It seems stupid to be this uncomfortable, but back then it seemed stupid to look less than Wow even when traveling – especially on the way to a new country and a new life. There would be new opportunities to be met, and I wanted to meet them fully prepared. I remember being shocked seeing professional women in downtown Toronto rushing to work in suits and sneakers. Back in Russia, in those days we only wore sneakers to the gym. I think Russian women wore high heels even on those long romantic walks on the beach that every second person on dating sites is talking about. Heels are a culture, a statement – a way of portraying sexuality and power. Of course, these days, I wear sneakers 90 percent of the time because of my busy, hectic lifestyle. But having had an operation on my leg left me without heels for six months and I struggled. It felt like some of my power and feminine energy were taken from me.

The importance of how we, as women, dress, walk and talk is often undervalued in modern society. Of course, some do spend a lot of money on clothes and heels, but there's also a trend to look "natural" so that others accept us "for who we are." And while that's important, it's still much more pleasant to look at a woman who's well-maintained. Why would you say that if she's well dressed, she's not herself? The way we dress and appear to the world is a reflection of what's going on inside. This is how we perceive ourselves, and it's how we want others to perceive us. If I put on a garbage bag, I'm acting like a rebel. I'm fighting against something or somebody. I'm at war; I'm in pain.

Loving me for who I am is important, but how I take care of myself is a big part of who I am. The part that loves herself gives herself value. She devotes time, money and energy to taking care of herself. She brings importance to her existence, and this means she demands that value is given back to her from the outside world. We need to be demanding to get what we want. We have to be "Miss Demand!" I respect how I spend my time and I demand that others value my time – not to be late, not to cancel at the last minute, not to look at Instagram when we're spending time together. It's the same with money. If I invest in my outside and inside improvement, I automatically show this to the world, and the world (and it's a man's world) gives it back to me in the form of gifts and pleasures. I think it's a two-way street: the more we pay attention to ourselves, the more attention we get. And we do love attention, don't we? We suffer when we don't get enough.

One easy thing we can fix right away that would tremendously improve our self-esteem, our self-confidence, and increase the amount of that attention, is to change how we walk. Have you ever seen a woman walk into a room straight as an arrow, with her head up? She looks confident, so sure of herself, so sexy. Is this really what she's experiencing? Not necessarily. She might be faking it, leading us to believe what she wants us to believe. You won't notice if she is skinny or not. To you, she looks hot – sometimes too hot for men to approach her, because they feel intimidated. That's the downside of being Wow. Men may think you must be in high demand, or that you just can't be alone. Or they may think, "Who am I to be with her?" That's why a lot of beautiful women are lonely. But if we choose to be outstanding, we must take those chances. In the end, there'll be one Wow man, who is equally self-confident and who won't be intimidated. He'll be proud of you and want to show you off. He's the type of man you want to be with anyway. Who needs unsure, insecure and fearful men? I don't.

A lot of our fear of aging is coming from the paradigm that we won't be attractive as we age. An aging woman is not perceived as attractive. Since there's nothing we can do about the natural process of aging, let's do everything in our power to be in high demand as we get older. (And mainly, to feel satisfied).

I'm lucky to have an outstanding example right in front of my eyes: my mother. I'm so grateful to have a role model who helps me understand that sexuality and attractiveness is not an age thing; it's an inner state. She hasn't had an easy life. It's been full of ups and downs, where she's struggled and suffered. Even so, she never lost her appeal and sexuality with age and the harshness of what life threw at her. She's a good girl from a good family. She married my father out of love, even though it was totally inconvenient.

He was from a very different social circle. He was young, poor and very handsome, but he was so charming that she became absolutely dependent on him mentally, physically and materially. While I know I said that to be totally independent is not necessary (if even possible), her dependency was way overboard, to my understanding. I guess being "all in" was her idea of being a good mother. In those days, the norm was that the man was the provider and the woman was the caregiver. At 40, she moved to Canada, where she realized that you can still be a good wife even when you actually talk and express your thoughts and views out loud.

Growing up, I saw the way she behaved, and I detested it. I hated it. I felt so bad for her that I made a decision not to be like my mother. I wanted to be as beautiful, but I promised myself I'd never give away my power. And then my father got sick. I already described the terrible disease that took away his movement. All of a sudden, I didn't see that weak, powerless woman anymore. She became strong and solid. She showed her strength in the unconditional love she had for him, despite all the pain he'd caused her. She took care of him to his last breath. She moved his heavy, immobile body. She helped him swallow, as he was losing nerve impulses, and couldn't do it on his own. To my great surprise, I saw a totally different woman, someone I admired and respected. She is the type of woman I wanted to be like – the Wow woman. I have to admit, I never learned to love anybody that unconditionally.

After my father passed away, she started living a different life. Actually, the only thing that changed was that she shifted focus back to her own needs. She started going to the gym and further improved her eating habits. A lot of women ask me if it's too late to start getting in shape after a certain age. When my major transformation at 42 doesn't inspire someone, I show them the photo of my 67-year-old mother. That helps a lot. It disappoints a lot, too, because it demolishes another excuse: "Oh, I'm too old to start." No, you aren't too old. You're just not important enough to yourself. It's as simple as that. Admit it.

My mom also has this enormous feminine energy and sexuality. She attracts men like I never could. (Much younger men, too). It's in the way she smiles at them, the way she talks, and how she holds her head a little to the side, as if she's really interested in what they have to say. Those little feminine tricks that are second nature to her are possible to learn, but it takes practice, like everything else. Remember the saying, "Fake it 'til you make it?" It works here, too.

I had a client who was lacking self-confidence big time. She always felt like a little grey mouse, not sure how to walk and talk. She was very well-educated, well-dressed, and had plenty of money, but her body showed all her inner insecurities. Her head turned to the side, and her shoulders scrunched forward. To the world, her message was, "I'm worthless. I have no value. I'm nobody."

What would the world give back to her? You get what you give. She couldn't manifest anything she wanted in life. If you want love and respect, show love and respect (to yourself, at least).

At our coaching sessions, every 10-15 minutes, I had to physically move her head back to a straight position, so she didn't look like she was apologizing for all the sinners in the world and begging for forgiveness. It took time, but we fixed it. We created the role of princess for her. She couldn't slouch and hold her head sideways, because her crown would fall off. She didn't want to lose her newly acquired crown, so she had to change. And her life has improved accordingly.

For some reason, we tend to underestimate the importance of body language. Some of us just don't care how we look to the outside world. Why don't we care? Why do we care about cars, houses, and even cats and dogs, more than we care about what we bring into this world? There's a message in everything we do and say, in every look and smile, and in our pink hair and blue nails. By the way, I used to hate blue nails. I thought that nail color was for younger, more liberated and rebellious girls. But to my surprise, my man happened to like blue nails. A few years back, being egocentric, super opinionated and a know-it-all, I would've said, "No blue nails allowed in my world." But as I get older, I realize that instead of knowing it all, I don't know anything. This position, plus my newly adopted "What if?" theory is helping me live and grow, enjoy and achieve. What if blue nails are not as bad as I thought? And you know what? Once I gave myself permission to try, I decided I love them.

Now I get a lot of compliments, and women send me photos with their blue color variations, saying I've motivated them to think differently. They thank me for that mindset shift, and I thank my man for it – for the reminder that I have unneeded paradigms.

I'm still not clear on how much men's opinions should influence our choices. There were times I did listen to men about how they wanted me to dress. One of them didn't like animal prints and short skirts, and another one hated pink and long dresses. Is that the same situation as with blue nails?

No. The difference is that I love animal prints and short skirts, so my needs weren't met. There was discomfort in it. With the nails, I listened, tried something new, and came to love it. Sometimes, we should just listen to our men – they do make some sense. Usually, our dislikes or likes are based on previous experiences or somebody else's opinion, but what if it's the wrong experience or decision? Listen to your man sometimes. Be smart and logical. If he likes those babushka-looking shoes on you, if they excite him in some strange way, can you wear them when he's around? Will you and your ego die in that hour or two? What if this would make him feel great? Don't you ultimately want to do that? You can always put on your super comfy running shoes later.

In spite of me being rebellious, I used to agree with men – not for the reason of making them feel good – but because I wanted to be liked and loved. Basically, it was a fear of losing him that made me so compliant. At the time, I wasn't feeling strong enough, and I fell into one of those love and fear traps. It was with the one who didn't like pink. Oddly, I met him a few years later with his next victim – and what a Miss Piggy she was. And not just because of the pink she was wearing, that he apparently hated. There were other reasons. Don't tell me we talk nicely about our exes and the new women of our exes. We don't.

When a woman is living her life constantly experiencing the fear of losing her man, she's being less than herself. Men are hunters. They have an innate need to hunt. It increases their testosterone level and sexual desire. When a woman experiences fear, it's not sexy or attractive. She is not as interesting to him. She's not as appealing. Feeling fearful destroys our Wowness. It almost destroyed me completely. When he decided to trade me for Miss Piggy, I ended up in a medical emergency. My fingers and tongue got numb, and I had difficulty breathing. The doctor was questioning me on my medical history, and I told him about my father's lethal disease.

Feeling almost dead already, I asked the doctor if he could make sure to first eliminate ALS, as some of the symptoms I had reminded me of how his illness had started. He described the feeling as some little mouse running all over his body.

"We can't," he said. "Most likely, that's exactly what you have." ALS: Amyotrophic Lateral Sclerosis. The deadly disease with no cure…

Have you ever been diagnosed with a terminal disease? I pray you never are. The type of fear you go through is difficult to explain, and absolutely impossible to forget. That fear paralyzed me. My legs went numb, and my throat got strangled. I was shaking, cold and nauseous.

Why didn't that general practice doctor at the Emergency just say, "Go see a neurologist to confirm or eliminate that diagnosis"? Why not? Was it medical ethics, or just his own stupidity and ruthlessness? I don't know. I know I asked for a tranquilizer or a shot of something to calm me down. "We don't have any in this department," they said. And with a $5,500 bill, they sent me home. Get medical insurance when you travel. (Or don't get attached to men – it's costly).

I never made it to a neurologist, as I started practicing self-help. "I am healthy and happy. I am healthy and happy." I was saying this mantra hundreds of thousands of times, trying to convince my mind and body it was true. I was slowly encouraging myself to accept that truth. First, my smart brain was not trusting me on this. *The doctor knows better and you have all the symptoms*, my brain was thinking. By the end of the day, though, I felt like the fear slowly wasn't as strong anymore, like I had managed to convince myself. Since this meditation calmed me down, I started looking for ways to treat myself. Somebody I knew referred me to a great Chinese doctor. I was lucky to get an appointment in a couple of days. He made some comments about how American doctors give out diagnoses like this pretty often, and he put lots of needles in my body. "Darling, you shouldn't take things this seriously," he said. "Men, especially. Don't take them seriously. Life is just a dream. Enjoy it. You won't die this time, that's for sure."

Whether you listen to somebody's opinion or make your own decision, there's no right and wrong on how we present ourselves to the world. We have a choice. But when we do choose, as in everything else, we may as well choose the image that we want to convey. Why wouldn't it be a beautiful message? Every masterpiece has a frame – a nice frame, too. Even though the painting is a piece of art by itself, the frame adds more value and beauty. You're beautiful as is, I know. Still, the frame will help. Like eyebrows – they add a frame to your pretty face. Never forget to fix your brows. It's a little, but important upgrade.

Voice is also a very important part of us. The tone, the speed, the pitch of your voice determines the message the listener gets even before they understand the actual meaning of the words. Personally, I don't like women who are very loud. Usually, they're very opinionated. They know everything, they argue. They especially like to argue with men – about everything. It's like they have to prove their existence and self-worth.

You'll never hear a queen, for example, argue and scream to prove her point. A Wow woman can use pauses in her speech, and talk slowly but firmly in order to be heard. She doesn't need to be loud. Feminine power is soft but strong. A woman can prove her point with just a look.

After one evening at the Ritz-Carlton Casino twenty years ago, I'm extremely careful about watching what, when and how I say something. It was beautiful, posh, and rich. I felt like I was in the movies: chic women in diamonds and rubies, and long dresses with fur palatines on their shoulders. James Bond-looking men in tuxedos. The air smelled like money, Roquefort cheese, wine, Foie gras and gambling tables. I looked Wow. I wore a long dress with high heels and had my blond hair teased high. It was one of those nights when I actually loved how I looked.

I'm not a great gambler, but I know some rules of Blackjack, like the fact that people playing are sensitive about the last hand. The whole draw may depend on whether the last hand takes the card or stays. Like any other game, it's not winning, but the process itself, that is exciting and adrenaline-driven. You get caught up in it, and some never come back to reality. There was this British couple playing last hand, and I love accents. Obviously, I have an accent myself since I came to Canada at 17. People tell me it's sexy. Honestly, I agree. But my striving for perfection and the need to fit in stopped me from a lot of great possibilities. I didn't speak much in law school. I haven't done very well at the movie auditions. I'd rather die than get up at a birthday party and make a toast. It's okay when you have nothing to say, but when you do, fear of public speaking is one of the worst fears. Of course, it's really the fear of being judged and rejected; it's a desire to be liked and loved. In my opinion, this should be the number one skill to learn in all schools, especially law schools. But at my two law schools, we didn't study that. Going on stage half-naked in my Swarovski bikini was the first step to overcoming that fear of being disliked and rejected by the general public, so the fear of speaking is now gradually disappearing. What a liberating feeling that is.

Back at the Casino, I wasn't afraid to speak. The champagne must have helped me overcome the public speaking fear. I was angry at the British couple for drawing a card when they were supposed to stay. "Darling, you got to let me know – should I stay or should I go?" They were laughing and having fun, and they were very annoying. The usually-adored British accent was very irritating because of the circumstances.

"You should have your cup of tea and go home," I said in Russian to my friend, and added a few other spicy comments. The woman turned to me and in perfect Russian, with British politeness, said, "So, you speak Russian?"

I was shocked. I was speechless. I was destroyed. I turned every color of red in the spectrum, and then turned white. I wished I could become invisible and disappear. Never, ever do I want to experience that feeling of shame. So now I watch what I say very carefully. If I don't have something positive to say, I don't say anything. You can't take back what you say – at work, in relationships, with children and friends. People may forgive us, but to forget is the tough part. It's hard to forget.

The outer Wow of me is as important as the inner. Anything that sends a message about me influences my relationship with the world. We can't control that world. We can't make it behave the way we want, but we can control how we communicate with that world. We impact our surroundings with the new, sexy, vibrant you, or you impact the hectic, dull everyday life of the people around you. That meaning we portray by the way we talk, walk, speak and dress – it all counts either towards our Wowness or away from it. If you can choose, why not choose wisely?

WOW WOMAN ACTION STEP 11

Think about the various components of your image that I've addressed above. How do you walk? How do you talk? How do you dress? What message are you sending the world and those around you? Is it a message you really want to convey? If not, how would you change it? How would you express yourself differently? Write out what you'd like to change. Would you walk differently? Would you move a little more slowly, deliberately? Would you tilt your head to show your interest? Only do it if you mean it!

_____

_____

_____

_____

_____

_____

_____

_____

_____

_____

_____

_____

_____

_____

_____

What about your speech? Would you talk more slowly? With less volume? Or talk more, so that people know you require attention?

_____

_____

_____

_____

_____

_____

_____

_____

What about the way you dress? Have those leopard spandex pants been getting too much play? How would you do it differently? What feels good? What's comfortable? How would you look so that when people see you, they know you were born Wow?

_____

_____

_____

_____

_____

_____

_____

_____

CHAPTER 12

Members Only: Your Club, Your Rules

What would you say if I asked you if you'd like to live on a boat? A big boat – let's say over 50 meters. A yacht, rather, with a British captain, a chef from New Zealand and Czech stewardesses all dressed in white uniforms, saluting and cheering you every time they see you? I bet you wouldn't mind. Or would you? I'm sure almost all of my readers would enjoy it. It's like a dream come true. It's a fairytale – and we want to feel like princesses. Most likely, you've seen this in the movies. The boat is docked in some town in the south of France, say Antibes or Saint-Tropez. You walk by this boat and see people on the sundeck drinking champagne and having fun. Music is playing and they're dancing away. They look like they have no worries, that their life is perfect. It seems like they don't have health or money issues, their children don't get sick, and their relatives don't die. Their life is totally perfect and complete. As you stare at that woman standing on the deck, blonde hair waving in the wind, who's looking at you through those Dior sunglasses, you're wondering who she is. Be honest: you envy her a little. You want to be like her. You want to have it all. (At once, preferably). You take photos of her, and you take selfies with the boat. You send them to your friends and relatives like you're a part of that worry-free life, and they envy you, too.

Most likely, you won't be invited aboard the boat, so you'll never know the truth. You'll never experience the feeling of standing there on the boat, looking at other "normal" people who are having real fun, taking pictures of those unattainable properties and unachievable dreams. People who are enjoying their days with friends, boyfriends, and colleagues have this privilege that they take for granted: they get to be around people they love and choose to share their happiness with.

Actually, I was that blonde on the boat. I was the one hiding my tears under the fashionable sunglasses, crying out loudly because of my loneliness. I was that "Lady of the Yacht" everybody was looking at, wondering if I was the owner of the boat named "Lady Yacht." In reality, it wasn't named after me. It belonged to a family member of my daughter's father. Because of some legal battles, this asset couldn't be disclosed, so the fact that I lived there couldn't be disclosed either. Imagine getting the royal treatment every minute of your life. You're asked with a rather annoying frequency what you'd like to eat, drink, and do. At first, it's a pleasure to be the master. Then you just want to go to the kitchen and serve yourself some eggs the way only you make them, but the chef shows up and insists on serving you. It's three in the morning! You feel bad and guilty for waking him and for being hungry, and you almost feel apologetic that you're being pampered. You try not to ask for any service, but they insist.

Think about it. You drop your fork and they run to get you a new one. Mention you want to go to Cannes, and they start the motor. What an irritating life that is. Indeed, it is. Really. You know why? Because you can't share it with anybody. You can't invite your friends. You can't let your enemies (if there are any), know of your success. Your social circle becomes the crew and the internet – but the internet aboard doesn't always work.

People are social creatures; we need other people. We need support and encouragement as much as we some-times need disapproval (and a kick in the butt) for some extra motivation. It doesn't matter if you're an extrovert or an introvert. A lot of our wins and losses depend on who we surround ourselves with. Oftentimes, we count on getting that much-needed support from our closest friends and family. Based on my own experience, though, it may work or it may not. Boyfriends, mothers and husbands don't want us to achieve more. They act like that reptile part of our brain, only wanting us to be safe. And that's not for us – that's not unconditional love. That's a pretty selfish thing. Their own existence feels threatened. They don't feel like there's a need for them to change, and we make a huge mistake by thinking they're also craving change and dying to join us on our one-way trip to Wowness. They may not be ready, as they don't have their Why yet. Your changes are dangerous for their well-being. They'll feel pressured to upgrade their own looks, health, life and attitude. That causes distress, and they'll try to talk you out of your crazy goals. It's not about you; it's about them.

If you don't get the support you need from those you expect it from the most, I know how you can get it for sure. Surround yourself with people who've already achieved what you'd like to achieve – those who've succeeded in what you've just allowed yourself to dream of, who you admire, who are your role models, who you want to learn from. Surround yourself with coaches or trainers who will take you by the hand and walk you from point A to point B without judgement or emotional involvement. Find a group of women who have been stuck like you are now, but succeeded in getting themselves moving toward an upgraded life. Find that team, and let them be your coaches.

When I all of a sudden decided to become an athlete, I surrounded myself with athletes. My new trainer became my best friend. Leonid Istomin. He's a legend on his own and deserves at least some words. He is a bodybuilder, an IFBB pro, who got liver cancer. His father and grandfather also both died from the same disease. They lived in Kazakhstan, close to the Semipalatinsk Test Site, also known as "The Polygon," which was the primary testing venue for the Soviet Union's nuclear weapons. He was about to die, but a true miracle happened, based on his strong desire to live, and a liver transplantation saved him. He came back very strong, and never quit bodybuilding. He never quit living his life to the fullest. I might be bragging a little now, but I feel very proud that I motivated him to come back and compete again. As we spent a lot of time together training, I got to know his deep desires and wishes. I knew he wanted that feeling of being on stage again. I made a decision to help him do it. And he did, because he's not just a cancer survivor; he's a winner and a real Wow man.

Another addition to my social circle was a girl I saw on Instagram. She was professionally competing in bodybuilding in the US. What attracted me to her was that she came to the States all by herself from a small town in Ukraine. She had no support or money and no obviously great bodybuilding complexion, yet she made her way up to the professional league. And she was already over 30 at the time.

I respected those achievements of hers, so I reached out to her and we met. I started spending time with her in LA, and then invited her to stay with me in Toronto. I simply copied everything she did. We ate together, trained together, went to photoshoots together. I was learning a different mentality – a winning mentality. I get a lot of questions about training while having those not-very-pleasant days of the month. Usually that's used as an excuse to skip a planned activity. I always think about her and laugh, imagining how she'd never say she was going to skip training because of her period.

Little by little, fitness trainers, competitors, and experts became my new social circle – my friends and family. They understood what I was going through. They could relate to how I felt when shredding, when stressed, and when hungry. They could give real advice, based on their own expertise and experience. I dove so deep into this new, totally unknown field to me, that I was approached by one of the leading magazines to go to the largest Fitness Exposition called "FIBO" in Cologne, Germany as a reporter. I guess my acting skills were pretty good, if people believed I was an expert. The Law of Attraction at work again! Little did they know, I was no expert. I didn't know who those bodybuilders were. Honestly, I faked it. I would go up to all the "IT" moguls of bodybuilding – Rich Piana (God Bless his soul), Shawn Rhoden, Cedric McMillan and Jay Cutler – and here I am, a newly born expert on body-building. *Breathe in, breathe out. Just do it, and something will come of it.* And it did, because it always does. When I'm in doubt and I want to be brave and bold enough to present myself as an expert in bodybuilding, I look at my stage pictures. When that's not enough, I have videos. You may call it bravery. You may call it confidence. For me, it's a new algorithm in life: *What if I can do it? What if I succeed?* And I go ahead and try.

Before this exhibition, I didn't know who Rich Piana was, but I needed to ask him something. I needed to chat to this freaky-looking man, the King of Synthol – an oil substance some inject in the muscles to look bigger – about some interesting bodybuilding stuff I had no idea about. I saw the name of the nutrition company he was representing. It was called 5% Nutrition. I asked him, in a rather joking manner, what that meant. All of a sudden, he became very serious, in great dissonance with those crazy blue-lensed eyes and overdone Synthol biceps. These deep, philosophical words were coming out of his mouth. He said that only 5 percent of people are ready to follow their dreams, ready to be persistent enough to reach their full potential and to fulfill their dreams. I had shivers. I felt like I totally understood what he meant and, to be honest with you, I felt like I was privileged to call myself part of the 5 percent and privileged to have met him. He died six months later.

I get asked a lot if we need a coach to reach our goals. I have no doubt on this matter. I'm positive we do. Every singer has a vocal coach. Every athlete has a sports coach. We all need somebody's expertise to get results. (That is, if we really want results). In reality, many don't actually need the results they're bragging about. They like the idea of wanting to want the results, but they don't want to be working toward their goal. They're enjoying thinking of a hypothetical outcome they could have theoretically achieved. These are the same people who aren't ready to invest money in their own personal development. They're scared to be defrauded and afraid of others making money on, as they say, their "pain points." Let it be. People are different. It's actually good that so many don't want to grow – it makes for less competition for us at the Wow level.

As I already mentioned, I consider Bob Proctor to be my coach. His book, *You Were Born Rich*, inspired the title of this book and the whole concept of us actually being born Wow until we were convinced to be otherwise. Also, the Law of Attraction has been my own law to obey for getting results.

To reassure you that the Law of Attraction truly works, I'll share with you some personal information. I was very strongly attracted to everything Bob Proctor teaches. I lived on Sprucewood Drive in Toronto, and Bob and his lovely wife, Linda, lived on Proctor Ave. Can you imagine? I hope Mr. Proctor doesn't mind me saying so, since this information is publicly available. Whether he chose the name of the street or the street was named after him, I'm not sure. You can ask him personally if you do his life-changing Matrixx program where he invites all the participants to spend the day at his house. Before you do that, though, I'll just mention that Proctor and Sprucewood are crossroads. We could basically see each other from our backyards.

Do you believe in serendipity? To my surprise, I never learned the word serendipity until a couple of years ago. I don't think I'd even heard it. I'm sure I had, but just never paid attention. In the dictionary, it's described as an occurrence and development of events by chance in a positive and beneficial way. My oh my, hasn't this been the story of my life! Even though I don't quite agree that they occur by chance. I think they happen to us because somehow, one day we made a decision for them to happen. These events happen and life is never the same.

The Law of Attraction, followed by a serendipitous chain of events, works amazingly well. I've attracted remarkable events and wonderful people that I could never have dreamt of. And I keep attracting more and more! It feels like I've mastered some laws again – this time, laws of life. As you study the theory of the Law of Attraction, the universe will give you the means to your goal. How could I have possibly visualized that the Law wouldn't just give me the things I wanted, but would give me the chance to personally meet and have dinner with one of greatest teachers of the Law itself, Mr. Bob Proctor and his wife, Linda? I saw the movie, *The Secret*, 10 years prior. Could I have imagined this? I guess I made a decision that was too bold to admit to myself.

A friend of mine, who I hadn't seen or heard from for more than 20 years, came back into my life by coincidence. But you know I don't believe in coincidences. I know it was a decision and an action that created the result. This friend is a former professional Canadian bodybuilder, who, introduced me to the world of bodybuilding twenty-some years ago. We went to New York to see my first bodybuilding contest. He introduced me to Dorian Yates, one of the top bodybuilders in history. I remember having dinner with the legend. I was watching him eat enormous portions of steak, eggs and potatoes. I was amazed by the size of that man and the size of his meal. I was studying him like he was an alien.

That friend of mine showed me what a real workout is. He taught me the proper ways of building my body. With his guidance, I built my quadriceps in a short time, because he trained me the way people are actually supposed to train – using your brain a lot. My legs grew so big that I stopped fitting into my jeans. I didn't like that feeling, but the stubborn me didn't listen when he tried to convince me that 80 percent of building the body of your dreams is nutrition. I hear this a lot from women who are trying to get in shape. They do a lot of cardio, sweat for hours, and go to the gym three or four times a week. Some of them even actually work out when they go. For most, however, it's selfie time in the gym. What they don't want to accept is the fact that until you manage your food, it's almost pointless.

Unfortunately, I didn't listen to him. I didn't want to accept that I was just deaf and ignorant. I blamed him for my huge legs. And I blamed him for the whole idea that it's possible for a woman to gain muscle without getting bulky. It was easier this way; it usually is. When we refuse to trust and take responsibility for our results, everything else is our own way.

By chance (or by choice), we met twenty years later. He was very surprised and proud of what I'd done. We could now speak the same language. People who have gone through a bodybuilding prep are different people. They understand each other on a different level. They've been through a strict diet, deprivation, strenuous exercise, mental breakdowns and emotional outbursts. It's like war veterans – they speak a different language and are not understood by others because of what they've gone through. My little war was over, and it was time to move forward. I told him that I didn't want to practice law anymore. The only law I wanted to practice was the Law of Attraction.

He casually mentioned that he could introduce me to Bob Proctor, who was a friend of his. I remember those words struck me like a lightning bolt. Now how can you tell me the Law of Attraction isn't real? I manifested someone in my immediate social circle who could help me with bodybuilding, and another expert to help me with the Law of Attraction. It was Bob who told me to write a book, and here I am. You see how the Universe works when we listen and choose to hear?

As I said earlier, everyone needs a coach, an expert, to help them succeed. You need to find somebody who can be your support and who can share your accountability – a person who won't judge you, but will motivate you when you are in need. But you've got to trust this person 100 percent to be able to work with them.

You should share the same values and be alike – similar age, comparable circumstances and life challenges. I remember when I was trying to find somebody who could help me get unstuck. I saw a lot of girls in their twenties promoting active and healthy lifestyles with perfect bodies, tight skin, and lots of energy. As much as I admired them, I just felt like I couldn't relate. I couldn't use them as my mentors because they couldn't possibly know what I was going through – the feeling of overwhelm, the fear of aging, the anxiety that it's too late to start, and my distress from being afraid that I couldn't juggle my everyday life challenges with this new time and energy-consuming lifestyle. How would a younger woman understand what it's like to have hormonal imbalances, or to raise a daughter without her father's financial support?

That mentor you're looking for doesn't have to be the greatest at what she does. I mean, she doesn't have to win the Olympics. You know why? Because your goal is not to win the Olympics. If it is, then find an Olympic champion.

I can introduce you to a few great ones in figure skating, gymnastics or, of course, hockey. If you're just trying to get out of an obliger role and start caring for your own needs so you can finally enjoy your life, though, then you need somebody who's only a few steps ahead of you and has already gotten their ass off the couch. They don't give Olympic medals for that, but you get your life back. I think that's valuable enough.

In order to have that support and accountability, be prepared to invest in yourself through that coach. I'm talking money. Dollars, Euro, Rubles – even crypto money will work, whatever that is. As humans, we'll go out of our way to justify something we paid for. Don't you sometimes buy a pair of shoes that become very uncomfortable by the time you bring them home? Do you feel like you now have to wear them? You bought them and spent money, and now you have to justify that expense. It's the same with coaching: the more we invest, the better the chances are that we'll perform. We're not stupid enough to invest in something that's not going to bring us dividends, right? And an investment in your happiness is the best one out there!

I manifested my mentors. I reached out and they showed up. You can find yours easily enough too. Go to social media or Google. First you have to specify your number one problem. What do you want? If you're trying to lose weight but sabotaging yourself, Google that. If you want to become visible and sexy again, research that. If you're struggling with self-care and self-love, you need to look for that. And if you want the whole package – you have me. They don't call me the Wow Woman Creator for nothing.

Lastly, don't forget that you yourself are the one who'll do the work. You. You'll work on changing your old ideas and beliefs, you'll be sweating off that unneeded layer of fat protection, and you'll be starting earlier and finishing later for your dream to come true. You'll work your ass off – literally. But I promise, you'll get your results. I know, I'm very predictable (or even irritating), with the way I finish these chapters. That's called consistency, and you'll need that to be confident, because you were born Wow.

ACTION WOMEN STEP 12

Think about what kind of club you can join to find your tribe. A gym or sports club? A tennis club or dance studio?

_____

_____

_____

_____

_____

What kind of support will your peeps give you? What will you do together?

_____

_____

_____

_____

_____

Write out a description of people you know who will support you. Are these family, friends, someone you met online? On social Media?

_____

_____

_____

_____

_____

_____

If you feel like you need more specialized attention, what kind of a coach would you like? Would it be a woman or a man? What kind of experience do they need? What kind of achievements? Do they need to be certified or should they look like they practice what they preach?

_____

_____

_____

_____

_____

_____

_____

_____

_____

_____

_____

_____

_____

_____

_____

_____

_____

_____

CHAPTER 13

Get Your Satisfaction! Prove Mick Wrong

Most of my childhood summers were spent in my family's dacha – a cottage just outside of Moscow, in a very prestigious town called Malahovka. At that time, only a very small percentage of the population could afford to have a summer house. In truth, only a very limited group of people were able to make money. The rest were getting paid a tiny set salary and a bonus at the end of the year. The bonus equaled a monthly wage and was called the "13th salary." Believe it or not, overall, people were pretty happy with the way they lived. They were led to believe that if they suffered a little now, later they'd have a bright, extremely exciting and blissful future. Of course, that was a big lie. That tomorrow didn't come for a few generations – but when you don't know any better, you're okay.

Sometimes I envy those people who live their lives and don't know how different life could actually be. Would it be a better life or not? That's the question, and we don't know the answer. But when you're not aware of what you're not aware of, you can actually be happy.

However, once we acquire more information on what we could've had, we tend to focus on what we lack. It's the feeling of not having that makes us incomplete and unsatisfied. If I didn't know, for example, there's a possibility of going to St. Barth's for New Year's Eve, I'd be happy to spend it at a local bar. Maybe it's better not to be aware, like Eve with an apple. If I hadn't savored Dom Pérignon, I might be quite pleased with Molson Canadian.

But I did; and so did my father. He realized that it was still possible to make money in a country where there was no private property and where you'd go to jail for having US dollars, so we could afford to spend some summer nights in the Russian Hamptons, if you will. The house my father built was a two-story log cabin with a traditional sauna called a banya built-in on the side. Everything was made of wood. It was very homey and comfortable, but not too safe for our belongings. At the time, crime wasn't as common as it is now. The most valuable thing in the house was the TV. That and some other personal stuff had to be protected – not from real thieves, but from drunks wandering around the village looking for something to steal and sell for a bottle of vodka. To protect these precious items, the builders installed metal bars on the windows.

My younger brother Alex, who hadn't been to Russia since his childhood, came to Moscow one day and we decided to visit the house where we'd spent our summers. My best friend, Julia, the Godmother of my daughter and her good friend came with us. It was mid-November and light snow covered the ground. It was pretty cold, and we drank lots of tea and warmed ourselves in the banya, beating each other with birch brooms.

We were having a great time remembering our childhood, and having some nostalgic moments. We made fun of the unskilled contractors who obviously didn't study any contractor safety rules and regulations. We decided to remove the metal bars in the morning.

I get up early. Thank God. It's a habit that's helping me a lot in life. This morning was no exception. I was having coffee and watching our TV that wasn't stolen due to the precautions mentioned above. Julia's friend Sasha got up and asked if I had any beer. Yes, Russians drink beer in the morning. We even drink vodka in the morning to feel better after last night's vodka. Honestly, it's quite bizarre to me that you need to drink more alcohol to minimize the hangover effect. Strange, but if so many people do it, there must be some truth to it. Or maybe it's just an excuse to attract more fun in your life the next day. I don't know. I don't drink vodka or beer. But thank God, Sasha did. I told him where the other refrigerator was. He went looking for it and came back looking worried. "Something's burning there," he said.

"Oh, it must be the *banya*. Don't worry," I told him. "It's not burning. It's the smell of burned logs from last night's Russian sauna experience."

"No, I think the sauna is on fire," he said, and ran out.

I immediately got up and ran to the *banya*. The only thing I saw were flames coming out the door. I smelled smoke. I ran up the stairs and woke my brother and Julia, screaming that there's a fire. It took less than a minute to get up and down. As I was coming down, smoke was everywhere.

Do you know that people don't die from flames? They die from smoke. In only a few minutes, it was harder and harder to breathe. I ran upstairs, wondering why my brother wasn't coming down.

Remember the metal bars? It would have been impossible to jump out the window from the second floor. If he didn't make it to the only set of stairs, there'd be no way out for him and the dog. Our wonderful American Staffordshire, Rocky, hid under the bed and didn't want to leave. Alex loved that dog. We all did. I screamed, "Let him stay. Let's get out of here!"

I guess Rocky was more afraid of my voice than the fire, so he went downstairs. As I rushed to the stairs myself, I realized that my car, my Mercedes, the only asset I took from my rich common-law marriage (besides the bronze statue of a Wow woman), was parked extremely close to the house. I knew it would be destroyed with it.

I remembered I had the keys in my room on the second floor, so I went back there. It was already impossible to see anything as my eyes were burning. I was losing it – my breath, my consciousness, my life. Holding the last breath of air in my lungs, I somehow managed to find the staircase, closed my eyes, and jumped down.

I remember feeling the need to breathe in, and I felt like I didn't know whether I'd take in air or if it would be my last breath. As I breathed, I found myself outside the house, on the snow, barefoot. I looked around. *Who's here? Did everybody make it? Who's missing?* All sorts of thoughts went through my mind. The house was on fire, but all four of us and the dog were safe.

Can you imagine how little time separated us from death? How close we were to the end of it all – all the suffering we go through in life, and all the problems we overcome in life? Five minutes. No more. This is how close you can be to the end, and to a new beginning (if you believe in reincarnation).

Five minutes from leaving behind those absolutely unimportant problems we give so much energy and importance. Five minutes from those blown out of proportion, unhappy events we create in our minds. Five minutes from the emotions we produce, live by, suffer by, and experience more drama from.

When the firefighters finally came, the chief asked how many were dead. He said it so casually, like he was asking his wife, "What's for dinner?" He was so used to casualties.

We didn't want to agree with the idea of burning ourselves alive. But in reality, isn't that what we do? We decide to finish our lives, sometimes before they even start. We decide to stop experiencing the taste of life and abstain from enjoying. We give up on living. We burn ourselves in the fire of everyday circumstances, putting the responsibility on our parents, society, or the government. We forget who we were once born to be and what we were supposed to experience – not achieve and do. We were meant to feel, taste and sense joy and delight. We were meant to feel the ecstasy of life, to feel life's orgasm. We were meant to feel sexy and free, the way life is supposed to be.

Once I lived through the near-death experience, life started to shine in a different light all of a sudden. Whatever felt extremely important lost its value. I stopped taking life so seriously. I started laughing at the things I was so worried about and made fun of the idiotic problems I created by myself and for myself.

I realized how much of that unneeded fuck I gave about unimportant things that I might not even remember the next day or month. I realized how much I worried and stressed over nothing, and how I dramatized everything and suffered. I realized how unimportant everything and anything is, except for the real things. I started appreciating my right hand and left leg. I acknowledged how lucky I am to be able to walk, talk and feel, and how privileged I am to see my daughter. Without knowing that she could've lost her mother in a second, she's happy to see me.

Everybody is so obsessed with searching for meaning in life, that life itself becomes a never-ending struggle. And in the end, you die. It could happen to me in five minutes. For some, it may come in one. It won't matter if you've found your meaning. Feeling is what you'll remember. Living an amazing and joyful life is the meaning of life to me. Helping others get a little closer to that life is the real meaning of life. Sharing your Wow with others, bringing light and happiness to the world – isn't this meaningful enough?

When you survive the fire, outlive your fatal diagnosis, or get out of life's problems alive, you feel grateful to everybody who has ever entered your life – anyone who, in any way, has influenced your growth or enhanced your path. Even those who made it difficult or threw stones at you had their purpose. You start appreciating life. You feel gratitude and love. This gratitude really is merely a shift in what you focus on. You won't stop having daily issues and your life won't become perfect, but you'll change. You'll be different. You'll be enthusiastic about your life because you'll finally get it. You'll understand it's a great privilege to enjoy and master your life.

We start appreciating things when we lose them. It's not just me and you; it's human nature. I was "lucky" enough to have these near-death experiences. Of course, I don't wish you the same. What I wish for you is to realize how grateful you should be to have what you already have – your health, your family, your children, your dog. Maybe it's your favorite coffee in the morning, even if it's a caramel latte from Starbucks with sugar, milk and hundreds of unneeded calories. Maybe it's your far-from-perfect, chubby, oversized body that somebody loves to hug and kiss at night. Maybe it's your not so well-paid work that brings joy and happiness to people. You have so much already. Feel that gratitude.

Instead, we choose to be stressed over life. Stress makes our lives less. It paralyzes our enjoyment and stops progress. We get sick mentally and then physically because of that little monster we create ourselves. Yes, we create our reaction to life events. We supply them a certain negative value and decide to spice it up with a particular dramatic emotion. How do you relieve stress? You choose your reaction, and action helps by shifting energy to the positive. Remember: being stressed is a choice. You can choose to do it or not. What's your choice?

Of course, there are a lot of practices to shift that energy to a gratitude state, like meditation, breathing, and repeating affirmations. They all work – but only if you do. What works for me is exercise. This is my meditation and an affirmation at the same time. Two for one, if you will. It helps me go through life challenges and keeps my ass in shape. Actually, it's really three for the price of one. Even better!

Based on my 45 years of experience, I realized an unpleasantly surprising fact: many of us don't know how to experience joy. Isn't that scary? I work with women who are achievers, leaders and front-runners. They have success and triumph. They've run marathons, built companies and made millions, but they don't know how to enjoy these things. They don't – and I'm one of them. I came to an awful realization in that search to achieve more and more. I lost the enjoyment of the process and got stuck in the rat race, but I don't want to be a rat. I'm afraid of rats. I want to be a Wow woman, full of feminine energy, sexuality and love.

Yes, sexuality. Do you know how many women have problems expressing it? How many of us grew up with the paradigm that being sexy is immoral? That if you want to be a successful lawyer, teacher or doctor, you're not allowed to be sexy? If you're a mother, God forbid you feel a little too sexy. We've been told sexuality doesn't fit into these roles. (Or, really, any role of a professionally successful woman). And then as successful high achievers, we're shocked when our relationships with men don't work. Why aren't they attracted to us anymore? we wonder. *How come? I'm a CEO/Olympic winner/money-making machine, but he's choosing an uneducated girl who has read no books on "How to be successful in life," "How to get what you want in 7 days," "How to…"* But she's full of vibrant energy, loving herself the way she is. She's happy with what she has. She's accepting her man without judgement, not trying to help him get a better job or make more money. She's not trying; she's experiencing gratitude. Her energy is different – it's light and positive, and that's what men really want. They want to have that lightness and positivity; they want a drama-free life. Yes, they want it the easy way. I know – it's hard for the ever-striving-for-perfection woman to understand. And no, it's not fair.

I know I lost a lot of my feminine energy diving into the bodybuilding world. Even though it brought me to a totally different level of existence in a lot of areas of my life, it took away that lightness, that vibe. Yes, it does look sexy on stage and I love my body and the photos of it. But behind all these beautiful images and the six pack abs, I was always hungry, tired, and stressed. How attractive is that? A stressed, overworked, shredded woman is not attractive. She's not sexy; she's tired and irritated. She can't possibly be wanted by a Wow man.

Balance is a skill to master. So many of us are trying to find that balance in life. It's a very valuable skill. But the definition of balance is perceived differently. What we're trying to balance is how we spread our time and energy over different aspects of life: health, career, finances, relationships, spirituality, personal growth, fun and joy, and our social circle. These are the main zones of our Wowness. One area has a tremendous effect on the others. They're all connected. In order to find that balance, instead of trying to allocate your resources to all these spheres simultaneously, I find it to be more efficient when we choose the most important part at the particular moment and invest energy there. Once you enjoy results in one area, work on another one. Then we tear ourselves between family and career, trying to find the other level of balance in this pair. For some, it may never occur. The real balance may be in handling the love triangle, where the third subject is you. It's between you, your family and your career where you will find the real harmony.

I'm not a big fan of multitasking. To me, multitasking won't get you great results in either task. I'd rather concentrate on one particular assignment in everything I do, solve it, and then move to the next. Multitasking is like being a dilettante. Even though you express interest, you don't become an expert. In other words, you're doing a little bit of everything – and nothing.

On my own wheel of balance a few years ago, I scored high on finances, relationships, career, social circle and personal growth. (At least I thought my personal growth was very advanced). But everything is measured by comparison. My health and body didn't score that well. My self-esteem and self-love weren't as tuned in as I wanted. It took me three years of tiny, everyday, little steps to get those particular areas of life to the level they are now. It's not ideal. It's not perfect. It's just better – not by somebody else's standards or society's rules, but by my own feelings toward it. Now I can honestly say I'm so grateful that I've done what I've done. I love how I feel about it now, absolutely in love with the results.

Meanwhile, bodybuilding is a masculine energy, no matter what fitness gurus tell you. As I was focused on building the body and enjoying the by-products of that process, another area of my life got slammed a bit: relationships. I let it go. I forgot. Actually, I didn't forget, but I was focused on something else. No regrets, though, as I don't know if it would've been possible to have both. The bodybuilding goal was more important at the time. I was spending more time with trainers at the gym than with my guy. At night I was dead. The thought of having to perform a wifely duty that I, unlike other women with constant headaches, loved doing, scared me. Therefore, I wasn't paying enough attention to his needs, and men want their needs to be satisfied. I think I am a man in that sense. I told you, bodybuilding left its mark, and it's all good. Having finished working on one goal, I now have different goals, to bring back that feminine energy – that lightness, that vibrance, that sexuality.

To achieve any goal, you just have to make a decision. Once you have, the plan of how to accomplish it somehow enters your life by itself. Honestly. It wasn't like I was sitting there Googling how to bring back that liveliness into my life. I just felt and knew I wanted to dance, and I chose belly dancing instinctively, without any logic. Only after I started looking for a belly dancing school around me, I read that belly dancing helps you get in touch with your feminine side – exactly what I needed at that particular moment! Then, as always, the Law of Attraction did the job.

Knowing that I work with female achievers (and over-achievers) and help them reach their Wow goals while experiencing fun and exciting endeavors, the owner of the largest dancing studio chain contacted me and offered me free private lessons at her studio. Not one or two, but twenty. And a private locker! She said she appreciates and respects what I do, and she wants to have me as a part of her dancing community. She has become part of my social circle. See how that works? My new work of motivating women to be Wow, to allow themselves to be phenomenal and do the impossible is very rewarding in all different ways.

Enough of me talking. I hope you got my message. The main point of this book was to show you the possibilities, and to let you know it's not over. You have all you need – the time, money and energy to start living your life the way you choose for yourself. Whether you're over 40 or under 25, you have it all, simply because you were born this way. You came into this world with all the instruments ever needed to feel joy and happiness. Think of it like your cosmetic bag; you know it has everything and more inside, but it's tough to find that very important item in the beginning. When you take some time and give it some effort, you'll succeed for sure. You also know that nobody else will ever accomplish your mission impossible for you.

The very best they can do is support you and cheer you on, but your bag is your world.

If you've read this far, you're my kind of girl. You want to be Wow, you want to be the star of your life. You're not shy about wanting to shine bright. You want to feel attractive and sexy, and you're willing to do the work to get there. This is the type of woman I want to have on my team. This is the kind of woman I want to learn from. Yes, I'm selfish; I want something from you. I want you to inspire and empower me. I want you to share your energy with me. I like that fair exchange. I cherish and crave that. I'm sure you're the same way. You respect that trade and appreciate its incredible importance.

I hope our exchange happens and we both benefit tremendously from it. Let's learn and grow! Let's break stereotypes and paradigms! Let's listen to ourselves and each other! Let's share our values and empower others! Let's just be, and enjoy that being. Let's be Wow – and let's have fun!

WOW WOMAN ACTION STEP 13

As I am writing this last exercise, you know what I'm thinking? I'm thinking that five months ago, I didn't know how to write a book. The idea of writing 40,000 words felt overwhelming. I'd be lying to you if I told you I knew what I was doing. I didn't. You know why? Because I'd never written a book before. Now I've done it, and in reading it over, I have to admit there are some parts I like a lot. There are others that I feel nauseous about. I catch myself going into that "striving for perfection" mode I've been warning you about. I feel so naked at times. I've exposed my life as I did my ass.

I wish this had happened earlier. I wish I had understood that it's normal to feel this way when you do something new in your life. You feel like you don't understand what the fuck you're doing. You feel like a fraud, trying to pretend you're a writer, trying to write in English as if you're a native speaker, and trying to teach like you're a renowned guru. Believe me – it all feels very awkward, the same way that sparkling bikini felt on my bare ass. New activities can feel extremely uncomfortable, but the new results are exceptionally exciting! It's really up to us to decide whether we want to sacrifice stability and "safety" to go through that painful phase, but get these amazing and satisfying results. I'm so grateful for the decisions I've made. I'm so excited to make new decisions, and I'm passionate about what I am about to do next.

I'm realizing that so many things I always thought were impossible are actually doable. The number one challenge now is to choose what that new breathtaking goal is. Let's see. Skydiving: done. Riding a motorcycle: done. Belly dancing: done. Writing a book: done. The body of my dreams is always under construction. Have the best daughter: mission accomplished. And I have a new hobby: DJing. Can you believe it? Yes, I mix music. It's not the most standard hobby for my age, but it looks sexy, so it feels that way too.

Hmm… what else? What if I shoot for *Playboy*? That's a challenge for a 45-year-old woman who was ashamed of her body until her mid-forties, and who grew up with a paradigm of Playboy Playmates being less than wholesome. However, we're here to change those old beliefs and old, archaic paradigms. What if I decide to enter some beauty pageant for women over 45 – Miss Canada, or Miss

Globe, for example? This would be something unthinkable for me as someone who could never accept using outside beauty and good looks to influence the world. But we have agreed that we're here to do what we want, even if it's outrageously bold. We're here to be Wow. If you ever forget that, contact me. If you need my support and a kick in the butt, I'm always ready to help. I'll put you through my "Stern Success System." I want you to be Wow, because you were born Wow.

It's your turn. Remember the contract you signed in chapter 5? Are you still performing it? I hope you are. If so, you're already becoming more Wow every day. Now, why don't you do something bold and crazy? What if you take off your underwear for a day and walk around like that? (Keep the rest of your clothes on, please). That's right: go commando. Or what if you take a couple of days off and fly to Paris? What if you take yourself shopping for things you totally don't need but absolutely want? Did you know you don't need to justify that to anybody? You don't need a reason to do that. You can do whatever you want to do, without the guilt trip, and without anybody's permission. (Okay, if you absolutely need permission, you have mine).

Write down what you plan to do.

Now express your gratitude to 10 people who have inspired, motivated or supported you. Thank them, write them, or call them. Send them a gift of some kind. This is so empowering. Trust me.

Then think about three people who were not as supportive and send them your love, without overthinking, without logic or reasoning. Just do it. They won't care because they'll never know, but you'll immediately feel the relief. You can practice this every day, or a few times a day, and you'll gradually notice how joy is entering your life. It will stay there for good, if you choose to let it.

Imagine that you're standing there on stage all dressed up, wearing your sparkling Swarovski-covered diamond dress. You absolutely need to shine and sparkle. You want to be on stage and feel like a star. You were longing for these lights, and for the packed theatre full of men and women, looking at you, applauding and screaming with admiration.

Your jaw is trembling, and your teeth are chattering. You try to smile since it's part of your performance. Of course, your legs are shaky, doing a tap dance in unison with your teeth. You look absolutely phenomenal. You are scared shitless and excited at the same time. You want that new life, and you're ready to step out. You've made the decision. Okay. Stomach in. Hold your breath, and keep smiling.

Here you are! It's the perfect day and the perfect time to finally start living the life you've been postponing until the right moment for so long.

You have a goal, and this goal is extremely compelling.

You want to be Wow. You know your Why. You absolutely know you can do it! Rub your hands together, and scream if you want. Breathe in and out. Take a step. Claim it. Own it. Be Wow.

Welcome to your Wowness. You know you belong here.

You were born this way. You were born Wow.

With love and gratitude,

Katia Stern

ABOUT THE AUTHOR

Katia Stern was born and raised in Moscow, Russia and moved to Canada when she was 17. She has since lived in Toronto, Miami, Monaco, Moscow and other countries due to her hunger for new experiences and interest in diverse lifestyles and cultures. She is a single mother of a very talented teenage daughter.

She calls herself a personal development junkie who has always been interested in figuring out how to live the best life possible. She went from a psychology major to getting a master's in international law, but found her true purpose coaching people on how to be Wow. She has since become a health coach, fitness nutrition and hormone specialist, fitness trainer and bikini competitor so that she could help women transform their bodies.

Later, she became a certified Jack Canfield trainer in Success Principles, and is co-authoring a book with Jack called *Success*, due to be published early next year. With all these accolades, she is helping women change their mindsets and old programming, so that they can get out of overwhelm and feelings of guilt and resentment, and finally fall in love with themselves, fulfilling their own bold desires and living in peace.

She is a firm believer that all of us were born Wow – capable, free, and enough – but we've been convinced by society, teachers, and parents to think otherwise. Her mission, using her energy and passion, is to inspire and motivate women to experience love and joy every day of their lives so that they can have a totally Wow life – vibrant and fulfilling! She is leading by example, and is now participating in the Mrs. Globe beauty pageant. She is Mrs. Ontario Classique and is going for the Mrs. Canada Classique title.

Katia calls all her clients 'Stars.' She thinks we are all starring in our lives and we are all deserving of our own Oscar. Her Stars call her the "Wow Woman Creator" because she is helping women create a new version of themselves – the Wow woman.

For more information
about Katia and *You Were Born WOW*,
please visit the following sites.

Website Katiastern.com

Instagram katia_stern_
#youwerebornwow
#sternsuccesssystem
#wowwomancreator
#wowwomanretreat

Email katia@katiastern.com

Facebook Katia Stern

Please contact Katia Stern for information about
private coaching or wow woman retreat

Giving a Voice to Creativity!

Your donation will give a voice to the creativity
that lies within the hearts of physically,
spiritually and mentally challenged children.

By helping us publish their books,
musical creations and works of art you will
make a difference in a child's life;
a child who would not otherwise be heard.

Donate now by going to

HeartstobeHeard.com

The children thank you!!

Made in the USA
Columbia, SC
21 May 2020